BEYOND THE NEW MORALITY
The Responsibilities of Freedom

Beyond
the New Morality
The Responsibilities of Freedom

GERMAIN GRISEZ
and
RUSSELL SHAW

BJ
1025
.G7

UNIVERSITY OF NOTRE DAME PRESS

NOTRE DAME   LONDON

Library of Congress Cataloging in Publication Data

Grisez, Germain Gabriel, 1929-
  Beyond the new morality.

  Bibliography: p.
  1. Ethics. I. Shaw, Russell B., joint author.
II. Title.
BJ1025.G7   170   73-17772
ISBN 0-268-00533-8
ISBN 0-268-00534-6 (pbk.)

Manufactured in the United States of America

The authors affectionately dedicate
this work to their wives:

Jeannette Grisez
and
Carmen Shaw

Contents

Introduction

We are proposing an ethics. But what is *ethics?* As we use the word, it means a philosophical study of morality, of the foundation on which morality is based, and of the practical implications of a systematic moral outlook.

In our view, ethics must start with a clarification of the fundamental notions of freedom, action, and community. Then it can move on to examine the question What is the ultimate distinction between moral good and moral evil, between right action and wrong action? An answer to this question only becomes practically useful, however, when we work out a satisfactory way of thinking through concrete moral issues: "Should I do this or that?" "Should I support this or that stand on a public issue?" Finally, once we are in a position to take a reasoned view on moral issues, we can ask and try to answer the question To what extent is it possible to close the gap, in our own life and in society, between the way we think things ought to be, and the way they actually are?

History studies many of the same questions as ethics,

but history looks at particular actions that have actually happened, while ethics is concerned with human action in general or with possible kinds of actions. Psychology and the social sciences also share somewhat the same subject matter as ethics, but psychology and the social sciences are mainly concerned with how human beings actually do act and how societies actually do work, while ethics concentrates on how persons ought to act and how societies ought to be formed and reformed.

Theological ethics (moral theology or Christian ethics) deals with many of the same questions we treat philosophically here. The main difference is that theological ethics takes the doctrines of a religious faith for granted, as a point of departure. A philosophical approach does not take any particular set of beliefs for granted. While it is impossible to question everything at once, the philosophical approach regards every belief and viewpoint as in principle subject to question.

Philosophy tries to answer the questions it asks by pointing to facts which anyone can observe and proposing arguments any reasonable person should accept. The nature of the questions philosophy asks causes it to appeal to arguments more than to facts. "Arguments" here does not mean contentious disagreements. Ethics, for instance, argues mostly in the sense that it proposes clarifications of the meaning of certain basic notions, such as "doing an act" and "morally good," and then draws out implications of these basic notions.

The roots of the ethical problem

The central problems of ethics present themselves to a philosopher today in a historical context. We cannot go into that context in detail. But it is necessary to consider briefly and very sketchily the deep historical roots of the ethical problems with which we are still dealing.

These deep historical roots are twofold. On one side is the Judeo-Christian religious tradition. On the other is the Greco-Roman humanistic tradition.

The Judeo-Christian religious tradition contains the belief that God is the creator of all things. The act of creation is pictured not as an accident, nor as something God had to do, nor as an effort on his part to fulfill some sort of need, but as a completely free act. This religious tradition also contains the belief that man is made in the image of God, and that man somehow possesses a freedom which resembles the freedom by which God creates.

The Judeo-Christian tradition is based on the belief that God freely reveals himself to mankind and in his revelation offers to human beings a special, personal relationship. The Jew believes that he is free to accept or to reject the Covenant proposed through Moses; the Christian believes that he is free to accept or to reject the Gospel of Jesus Christ: although, of course, each also believes that he ought to accept the Covenant or the Gospel.

Thus for those in the Judeo-Christian tradition man has freedom of self-determination. He can make or break his whole existence by his own act, by his own free choice, just as God was able to create—and could as well not have created—by his own free choice.

When the Bible deals with moral good and moral evil, with what is right and what is wrong, however, it undertakes no general explanation of these concepts. The Covenant and the Gospel contain specific commands, which are represented as the will of God. The Bible always assumes that the fulfillment of divine commands will work for man's good. But it makes no extended attempt to explain why this should be so, beyond the fact that man's well-being depends upon his friendship with God, his creator.

The Greek philosophical tradition worked out various conceptions of what man is. Each of these conceptions of human nature served as the basis for an ideal of human life. In other words, the Greek philosophers developed conceptions of what man should be, and how an individual should live his life in order to measure up to this ideal.

The Greek philosophers disagreed considerably in the details of their conceptions of ethics. But they agreed on several points. 1) That there must be one ideal pattern of human life. 2) That rational inquiry should be sufficient to reveal this ideal. 3) That the ideal is based in human nature, not in individual preferences or divine commands. 4) That individuals fall short of the ideal either because of defective heredity (for example, slaves are just naturally inferior), or because of bad upbringing (for example, children brought up in a barbarian culture can only be semi-human), or because of lack of knowledge of what is good.

In short, the Greek philosophers developed very definite ideas of what man must do to live a good, fully human life. These ideas were proposed on rational grounds, as corresponding to the requirements of human nature. But the Greek philosophers had no place in their thinking for the idea of freedom of self-determination.

Throughout the history of Western culture, thinkers have been trying to join into some sort of harmonious whole elements from the Judeo-Christian religious tradition and elements from the Greco-Roman philosophical tradition. If one takes from the Judeo-Christian tradition the idea that man has freedom of self-determination and from the Greco-Roman tradition the idea that there must be a reasonable basis for judgments of moral good and moral evil, of right and wrong, one has the parts of the puzzle that ethics confronts.

Divine commands are not in the picture for ethics, since it cannot proceed by taking for granted particular religious beliefs. At the same time, much of the fixity of human nature that was taken for granted in the Greco-Roman philosophic tradition is removed, because we have come to take for granted the freedom and the dignity of the individual person.

An adequate solution to the puzzle of ethics, therefore, must do full justice to the fact that man has freedom of self-determination—that we determine the worth of our own lives. At the same time, it must do justice to the fact that we have real moral responsibilities, that there can be good reasons for judgments of right and wrong. It is not acceptable either to deny man's freedom or to treat moral requirements as the result of arbitrary human preferences or inexplicable divine commands.

Why ethics is important

Every child is brought up with a certain moral viewpoint, which is conveyed to him as much by action as by words. Small children take for granted the rightness of the morality in which they are being raised; they may not obey it, but it does not even occur to them to deny its reality and validity. At some point in adolescence or youth, however, most individuals in our culture become aware that they can either keep, amend, or even replace the moral outlook in which they were brought up.

These options are extremely important, because the framework of one's whole life is at stake. It is unfortunate if such a basic decision is made whimsically, or simply on the basis of rebellion against the viewpoint in which one was brought up, or merely by conforming to the prejudices of one's class and age group. A person's basic moral stance should be the subject of his or her most careful inquiry and most critical judgment.

The study of ethics provides an opportunity for such careful inquiry and critical judgment. If one is not going to turn his life over blindly to the old morality or to the new morality or to the opinions of one's friends or to the demands of one's feelings, he must think things through.

The only way to do this properly is to do it for oneself and from the ground up.

The present book is not offered to its readers as a substitute for such personal thinking. The viewpoint it advances is proposed as one alternative—among many—to be seriously considered. The authors think it deserves consideration because, frankly, it is the outcome of their own personal inquiry and reflection, and they are convinced of its soundness. But we do not ask anyone to believe what we say. We ask the reader only to examine the questions discussed here and to consider the reasons we give for our views.

If a person has a deep and personal religious faith, he may not feel that it is necessary for him to undertake the sort of reflection in depth that we are proposing. We cannot agree with this point of view, even if the religious faith in question is one we ourselves share. A religious person need not reduce everything he believes to reasons, but he needs to assure himself that his act of faith is itself morally defensible in human terms. Moreover, one can hardly think out a sound theological ethics unless one has worked through the problems the philosopher must face.

Furthermore, the study of ethics has an importance that goes beyond the individual and his personal life. We live in a society that is pluralistic, a society in which there are disagreements about basic issues. When we find ourselves at odds with our fellow citizens on matters of public policy, we cannot rest on an appeal to our beliefs which our fellows do not share. In this context, we must be ready to give good reasons for our judgments as to right and wrong, for our views about what is humanly good and bad.

Only by thinking through our own fundamental outlook are we in a position to articulate the strongest possible case for our judgments. Of course, even if we understand ourselves, it is altogether possible—even probable—that we shall be unable to convince others by philosophic arguments alone. But where fundamental issues are at stake, it is worth the effort. For what is the alternative? Propaganda, which is a kind of violence to reason; and, when the universal use of propaganda renders all propaganda ineffective, the final "argument"—outright physical violence.

No one who cares for others and respects himself wants to use violence to put across his views. Thus, even if ethical reflection does not seem very likely to lead to agreement in a pluralistic society, it is worth trying. Many disputes settled short of violence and without fundamental agreement in our society are worked out by compromise. If we are going to negotiate the compromises most acceptable to our own convictions, it is necessary, once again, that we understand our own positions and our reasons for them.

Thus ethics has a vital role to play in our personal lives, so that we really can take possession of ourselves. And it also has an important place in our lives as members of a pluralistic society.

The nature of this book

It will be clear to any reader, and especially to professional philosophers, that this is not a technical work of philosophy. This is not said defensively, but only as a caveat to those who might otherwise approach the book expecting from it what it does not pretend to offer. One of the authors, Grisez, has set forth his ethical theory at length and in the language of technical philosophy in other publications and will probably continue to do so in the future. Professionals are urged to consult these expositions for a statement of the theory and examples of its application, in terms to which they are accustomed.

For whom, then, is the book intended? The primary audience is the college ethics class, where a teacher can supplement the book's presentation with that degree of technical and professional sophistication he or she deems appropriate. In the authors' minds, however, the audience for this work is by no means limited to students in college classes. Others, such as adult study and discussion groups, will find it useful. In addition, it is the authors' hope that the serious reader, reading independently, will study and reflect on it.

Obviously the present work does not attempt to set forth a variety of views; it is not a history of ethics nor an overview of the field. Rather, it seeks to state clearly and simply—in language comprehensible to the nonprofessional—a particular approach to ethics. For this reason it may well be read in conjunction with other works which propose other approaches.

For all audiences the "questions for review and discussion" and the list of readings at the end of the book provide an additional dimension. The questions are not meant to catechize readers but to encourage them to engage in further exploration of the issues raised and further evaluation of the answers offered here (as well as other answers offered by other ethical systems). As for the readings, they do not comprise a comprehensive bibliography of ethics since such bibliographies are readily available elsewhere. They identify instead two kinds of sources: those which complement and/or develop at greater length particular points made in the text; and those which illustrate points of view with which the theory proposed takes issue.

The plan of the book

The best way to determine how the argument is developed is, naturally, to read the book. What follows is meant only as a brief look-ahead to those who may wish such assistance.

We begin with freedom, since the question of moral

good and moral evil is a question of freedom—how it is used or abused. Freedom, however, cannot be understood apart from action; and our analysis distinguishes three separate levels of action, with a particular "freedom" associated with each. Our principal concern is with the third level of action (self-determination) and its corresponding freedom, since it is at this level that one can speak most properly of moral good and moral evil. We note, further, that the individual as a moral entity does not exist in isolation; relationships with other people are part of the fabric of life, and hence ethics must deal with the community dimension.

All this, however, is only groundwork for the identification of principles by which one can determine whether an action is morally good or morally evil. Rejecting the solutions of relativism and subjectivism, we argue that the fundamental criterion is the manner in which one makes his free, self-determining choices. In chapter nine we identify two ways of choosing—"exclusivistic" and "inclusivistic"—and conclude that the second mode of choice is the morally good one because it leaves a person open to continuing and ever-greater growth as a person.

Next we move to the identification of guidelines which help one to choose rightly. First utilitarianism is rejected, because it locks one into an immoral pattern of choice. Instead, eight "modes of responsibility" are identified (in chapters eleven through thirteen) as guidelines for choosing, as well as for analyzing action. The problem of "ambiguous" action is examined in chapter fourteen, and a solution proposed in terms of the modes of responsibility.

The final section of the book applies what has gone before to several matters of particular concern, such as education, social reform and revolution, and theories of individual and social progress. The special role of religion in regard to morality (is it a help or a hindrance?) is considered at some length. The book ends with a brief description of how a person who wishes to do what is morally right might structure his life.

As will be apparent at many places, this book is concerned in a special way with the "new morality." The new morality means different things to different people, but the general idea is that traditional morality put too much emphasis on inflexible general rules, on obedience, and on abstract ideals of right and wrong. The emphasis of the new morality is on the concrete situation, on love, and on the person.

We are sympathetic on the whole to the intentions of proponents of the new morality. But we are not satisfied with the positions they have worked out. We do not suggest a return to the old morality; that is in any case no longer possible. Rather, we suggest an advance beyond the new morality, an advance toward a sounder and more humane ethics. The new morality is only a halfway house.

The ethics we propose here takes full account of the concrete situation, of love, and of the person. But it also seeks to put the concrete situation into the context of the whole of a person's life; it seeks to show how love requires a free response to human goods, a response which generates responsibilities; it seeks to defend the person and the community of persons against all the implications of theories and attitudes that would make of them mere objects, mere means.

*   *   *   *   *

Every work resulting from collaboration naturally raises questions in the reader's mind. Who is responsible for which idea or ideas? Who wrote what? Does the book reflect thoroughgoing agreement or a series of compromises?

One of the authors of this book, Grisez, is a professional philosopher; the other, Shaw, is a professional writer. The ethical theory set forth here is, properly speaking, Grisez's. However, the authors have discussed ethics with each other on a number of occasions over the past several years and have arrived at a substantial harmony of view. In addition, they have worked together on several writing projects involving ethical issues prior to this one.

The present book came about in the following way. Grisez's college ethics course for an entire semester was tape-recorded and transcribed. Grisez also drew up an outline of a short book on ethics (more or less this book). Working from the transcript and the outline but retaining considerable independence as to the ordering of the material and the manner of stating and illustrating concepts, Shaw produced a manuscript. The authors conferred and revised, added and subtracted. The result is the book as it now stands. The authors regard it as a joint enterprise, for which they are willing to share not only blame but (they hope) also praise.

1: Freedom Means Responsibility

Freedom. Everybody wants it. Poets praise it. Statesmen promise or proclaim it. Some men have given their lives to win it for themselves or others.

But what is it?

The word "freedom" can have many different meanings. It can refer simply to the lack of physical constraints. It can mean the absence of external social pressures and demands. Or it can signify that state in which an individual is able to create his own life—and, in a real sense, his own *self*—through his choices.

It makes a difference what kind of freedom one is talking about. They are not all alike, and they are not all equal. The freedom to determine oneself by one's own choices is the freedom most proper to a human being. It is the freedom with which ethics is most concerned.

Because there are different kinds of freedom, and because some are more properly human than others, it is worth looking at them in some detail, in order to see where they are different and in what each consists.

1

"Freedom" is physical freedom

The simplest kind of freedom is the absence of physical coercion and constraint. This is what we call "physical freedom." It is the kind of freedom enjoyed typically by wild animals ("Born Free") and by infants. Even inanimate objects can have this kind of freedom; we speak, for example, of "freely falling bodies." By contrast, a prisoner in a cell does not have freedom in this sense because he is physically prevented from leaving. Someone who is forced to perform some physical action, or physically prevented from doing so, is not acting freely in performing or not performing the action.

Physical freedom corresponds to the simplest kind of action, that which can be performed even by an animal or an infant. A dog chases a rabbit. A baby crawls across a room to get a red ball. In such action the meaning of the behavior comes from its culmination. And the behavior and the meaning are closely united. The behavior only makes sense in terms of the culminating performance (catching the rabbit, getting the ball).

In such action, freedom is present only in the sense that the behavior cannot take place unless the individual is not physically constrained. When there is constraint, there can be no action; when there is no constraint, the action can be performed. The latter situation represents physical freedom.

This kind of freedom is always a matter of degree. Some measure of physical freedom is essential if one is to act morally. (Acting "morally" here does not mean doing "what is right." It only means acting "in a way that *counts*—as right or as wrong—in moral terms.") At the same time, however, absolute physical freedom is not required for moral responsibility.

As a matter of fact, it is nonsense to speak of "absolute physical freedom." Everyone is subject to some physical constraint—the law of gravity would see to that, if nothing else did. Freedom in the sense of "physical freedom" is always more or less.

"Freedom" is doing as one pleases

"Freedom" can also mean doing as one pleases—the absence of social demands and restrictions. A slave's basic condition is not one of freedom in this sense, because what he does and does not do is determined for him by someone else, his master. By contrast, Robinson Crusoe was totally free to do as he pleased until Friday appeared on the scene. Since there was until then no one else to impose demands and restrictions on him, he enjoyed complete freedom to do as he pleased.

As is the case with physical freedom, so freedom to do as one pleases corresponds to a particular sort of action. This sort of freedom is proper to action done as a means to an end which is separate from the performance itself—action in which the end sought is not in the culmination of the performance. A clear example of this kind of action is planting seed in order to harvest a crop. Enjoying the crop is the end which is sought; but it is very widely separated, in time and in other ways, from the performance of sowing seed.

At this level of action, one is free to do as he pleases to the extent that he desires the end to be achieved and that the means is necessary to achieve the end. The grain-crop example obviously fulfills the second condition because there will be no crop unless the seed is planted; as for the first condition, it is fulfilled in the case of a farmer who plants seed because he wants a crop; it is not fulfilled in the case of a slave who plants seed only because his master tells him to.

Several things are characteristic of action at this level. For one thing, calculation—reflection on what means to employ in order to achieve certain ends—is both possible and necessary. Also, it is clear that doing as one pleases and responsibility are in opposition to each other. Responsibility in society is something that is imposed on one by other people. Freedom to do as one pleases is the absence of such imposition. One would be totally free at this level of action if he had to do only those things necessary to achieve the ends *he* wanted to achieve.

Immature people tend to think that this is the whole meaning of freedom. Freedom is doing as one pleases; it is the opposite of doing as one is required to do (by parents or other people in authority). A more mature view of the matter, however, suggests that this sort of freedom is not an unqualified good.

Some degree of freedom to do as one pleases is certainly essential to moral responsibility. However, unlimited freedom of this sort is impossible—and would be undesirable even if it were somehow possible—for anyone living in social relationships with other people. If people did not have responsibilities to one another, if everyone went his own way and did his own thing, society would collapse.

What is more important than unrestricted freedom to do as one pleases is that an individual be able to participate in appropriate ways in setting up and directing his relationships and the communities which make demands and set restrictions upon him. People have a right to have a voice in setting the rules of the societies in which they live, but this is a very different thing from opting out of all societies entirely in order to have maximum freedom to do as one pleases.

Ideal freedom and political freedom

Before passing on to the kind of freedom which is most important to ethics, it is worthwhile at this point to mention two other meanings of the word "freedom"—freedom in the political sense and ideal freedom.

"Political freedom" suggests a kind of freedom to do as one pleases which applies to nations rather than to individuals. In this sense a colony revolts and fights for its freedom.

There is, however, another sense of "political freedom"—namely, the participation of individuals in directing their own polity, which we mentioned at the end of the previous section. This concept is best expressed by the phrase "government by the consent of the governed."

Political freedom in this sense is closely related to individual freedom to do as one pleases. The difference is one of emphasis. In individual freedom to do as one pleases, the emphasis is on absence of requirements set by others. In political freedom the emphasis is on the fact that a person acts according to laws that he himself somehow shares in making. In addition, political freedom is concerned, not with the whole of one's life, but only with the part of it in which one acts as a citizen.

"Ideal freedom" refers to the freedom possessed by individuals and societies which are able to act in an ideal manner. This is a sense in which the word "freedom" is used by such different thinkers as St. Paul and Freud. St. Paul considered the sinner not to be free because the sinner is bound by reason of his sin to fall short of the ideal of uprightness; by contrast he held Christians to be free because their redemption from sin by Christ freed them for uprightness. Similarly, for Freud the neurotic is not free; but the cured patient, who has been liberated from his neurosis, is to that extent free to behave in an ideally healthy manner.

Although ideal freedom and freedom to do as one pleases can sound like complete opposites, they can also be seen to be compatible. Ideal freedom means that the individual is not blocked from doing as he ought to do; freedom to do as one pleases means that the individual is not blocked from doing as he wishes to do. However, most ideals of human behavior are put forward with the assumption that once one reaches them, an individual will find it easy and pleasant to fulfill them, and will actually wish to do so.

As for the content of ideal freedom, it varies widely, as there are diverse conceptions of the ideal condition of the human agent and diverse views of the obstacles to the fulfillment of these ideals. For Marx, for instance, the ideal human condition is attainable not by isolated individuals but only by society as a whole. However, the general concept remains the same: human beings will have ideal freedom when they can act as they ideally ought to do.

If one's ideal for man includes the requirement that he realize himself by his own free choices, then ideal freedom will be closely related to the most important sort of freedom, which we discuss next.

"Freedom" is self-determination

"Freedom" also refers to self-determination—the shaping of one's own life, one's own *self,* by one's own choices. This is the kind of freedom most closely related to questions of morality. To the extent that we can determine for ourselves who we shall be, we are responsible for our lives.

Self-determination means that, despite all external pressures and prior causes which can and do influence our choices, we retain at least some options of choosing or not choosing, of choosing one thing rather than another. In cases where there is no such option there is no real choice and no real self-determination. In such cases there is no question of "moral" action at all. When a man does something without really having chosen to do it, he is not acting either morally or immorally; his action simply has no moral quality. It is certainly possible for people to act in this way, and in fact they often do. But it is also possible for people to act on the basis of real choice and, in doing so, to be self-determining.

As with physical freedom and freedom to do as one pleases, so also self-determination corresponds to a particular kind of action. At this third level the action derives its meaning from a good in which one participates by performing the action. The action's meaning does not come from its consummation (first level—physical freedom) nor does it come from a specific goal the action is meant to achieve (second level—freedom to do as one pleases). Rather it comes from a purpose in which one participates precisely through performing the action. This purpose does not come at the end of or sometime after the action. Instead, it is present in the performance all along, at every stage. In this kind of action one realizes a good by participating in it.

Consider an example—studying simply for the sake of learning. Studying is the action. Learning is the purpose or good. It is obvious that learning is not something which occurs or is achieved only at the end of studying. Learning goes on all the time one is studying. One participates in this good all the time one is performing the action.

From this same example it becomes apparent how one and the same action can, simply by a change of perspective—or, more accurately, by a change of intention—move from one level to another.

First of all, all actions, even the most complex, can be broken down into their individual first-level components. In studying—reading a chapter in a book, for instance— your eye moves from one line of print to another, and from one page to the next. This simple process of looking at the words on the page is activity at the first level of action.

The same act of studying can also be an action at either the second or the third level. It will be an action at the second level if, for example, one is studying only as a means to an end—passing an examination. But studying will be an action of the third level if it is performed not to achieve some ulterior objective (passing a test) but for the sake of participating in a good (learning) which is intimately and inextricably linked to the action itself. As the example suggests, the same act can be an action at the second and at the third level at the same time—if, for instance, one is learning while he prepares for an exam, and is concerned about both purposes at the same time.

Determinism

Some theories of human behavior, which go by the general name of "determinism," hold that there is really no such thing as self-determination. They argue that all behavior is determined by factors prior to the choice. Many philosophers of the past three centuries, and especially of the nineteenth century, thought that belief in self-determination was unscientific.

This type of thinking is still influential in sociology and psychology, but it no longer has clear support from contemporary physical science and contemporary logic. Basically, determinism comes down to saying that every action is determined in advance; that everyone has to act as he does (for instance, because of his psychological makeup) and could not choose to act differently.

While determinism is not a true or adequate explanation of human action, it does reflect some perfectly accurate observations about some aspects of human behavior. For one thing, it is entirely true that antecedent factors play an extremely strong role in much behavior, a stronger role than many people are ready to admit. Some of what passes for free action probably is really not free at all. It is only as we have gained insight into psychological conditioning—how it occurs and how it exerts its influence—that we have come to understand this.

The concept of self-determination—of freedom at the third level of action—does not mean that action takes place without causes that precede it, or that the causes do not have a conditioning influence on the action. It does mean, however, that although antecedent factors certainly influence our actions, nevertheless we are not entirely determined by them in every case in which we choose an action. Not everything we do is a free, self-determined action; but for the average individual it is at least possible sometimes to perform such actions.

Experience points to the truth of this. If all of our actions were determined in advance by antecedent factors, we would not have the experience—often very intense and uncomfortable—of unsettledness and indecision in making a choice. There is no reason for deliberation about actions which are already determined in advance. Furthermore, when a person makes a choice, he does not experience it as something that *happened to* him but as something he *did*: "I made up my mind." The experience of choice is an experience of acting, not of undergoing. Determinism has to try to explain away our experience that what we are doing is really up to us.

Determinism also defeats itself. Determinism denies the notion of unconditional obligation, because it holds that all actions that would fulfill unconditional responsibilities are determined by antecedent conditions. At the same time, however, it is impossible to propose determinism as a point of view that ought to be accepted without assuming the existence of at least one unconditional obligation— namely, the obligation of being reasonable enough to accept the point of view proposed by determinism. In claiming that his theory is true, the determinist is saying that we *ought* to accept it, that we *ought* to accept the determinist's view that our experience of self-determination is an illusion. But it makes no sense for the determinist to tell us what we *ought* to do if we have no choice about it anyway.

Finally, and very important here, determinism is really beside the point as far as ethics is concerned. Ethics deals with the practical side of life—with what one ought to do in a specific situation. And while it is possible to be a determinist about someone else's action, it is impossible to be a determinist about one's own action, while one is practically involved in deliberating and making up one's mind.

Everybody has the experience of having to make choices—to choose one course of action or another. Determinism is of no help at all in the practical matter of choosing, because it holds that there is no such thing as real freedom of choice. This may be an interesting theory, but it is simply irrelevant when one is faced with the necessity of making a serious choice and making it here and now.

When, for example, it is a question of cheating on an examination and passing the course, or not cheating and probably failing, one does not get much help from the determinist's cheery counsel: "Whichever choice you make was determined for you before you made it." Rather than helping us make choices, determinism simply denies that we have any real choices to make.

Questions for review and discussion

1. Make up, or find in other sources, examples of the use of the word "freedom" in each of the senses distinguished here.

2. The word "responsibility" has different senses corresponding to three of the senses of the word "freedom"—namely, physical freedom, freedom to do as one pleases, and freedom of self-determination. What are these three senses of "responsibility?" (For example, what is the difference between saying that one's pet cat is responsible for the scratches on the table top and saying that a person is responsible for his own life?)

3. When we feel that we don't want others to boss us around, what kind of freedom is it that we want?

4. We shall see later that moral responsibility is not just a set of rules to be obeyed. However, supposing that *were* all there is to morality, would it be incompatible with freedom of self-determination?

5. Many people who hold a determinist position nevertheless insist that we are able to act freely. What do you think they mean by this position (which, incidentally, is technically called "compatibilism")?

6. It has been suggested that the idea that people have freedom of self-determination originated in the Judeo-Christian conception of man as made in the image of God. Leaving aside the question of whether you do or do not accept the biblical account, discuss the plausibility of this historical supposition.

7. Identify, analyze, and evaluate other arguments for or against freedom of self-determination.

2: Being a Person
Is a Lifelong Job

We looked closely at freedom in the last chapter, especially in order to distinguish "freedom" used to mean self-determination from other senses of the word. Self-determination is at the heart of the matter that concerns us in ethics. Now we are ready to go into greater depth in an attempt at understanding what freedom of self-determination is, and how it works.

Life is full of problems, but there is one problem which is common to every man's life—a problem whose solution gives meaning to life. It is how to be a person.

That is a deceptively simple statement. It says more than it seems to say. There are, after all, a number of false notions about human life which go to the fundamental question of what life is all about. When one says that the problem, the challenge, and the meaning of life lie in being a person, one is also rejecting several contrary views about life.

One contrary view is that the basic problem shared by all persons is how to *remain* persons. Another is that the fundamental challenge is how to *become* persons. The contention here is that it is a question, not of remaining or becoming, but of being.

Remaining a person is not the problem

Non-persons have a definite, given character. They are not self-determining but determined. To be fully themselves they need only remain themselves, something they usually have little trouble doing. As a writer once remarked so well, "a rose is a rose is a rose." A rose remains a rose; it is in no danger of becoming a dandelion or a turnip.

This is true even in the case of non-persons which are capable of acting and changing. Chemicals act and react; plants grow; animals perform in many different ways. In none of these cases, however, is real choice involved. Even animal behavior, which can be very complex and, as we say, "almost human," is not self-determined action.

It is instead a series of naturally determined processes whose meaning comes from the naturally given consummations to which the behavior leads (action at the first level). An animal does not enjoy freedom of self-determination. It does not choose how it will act; its "choices" are, instead, entirely determined for it by its own instincts and training, and by circumstances over which it has no control, so that in a true sense it cannot act other than it does. Nor is an animal self-conscious; it has no self of which to be conscious.

The point is that a non-person (a rock, a plant, an animal) perfectly fulfills itself by remaining what it is and by undergoing whatever changes happen to befall it. It does just what comes naturally, but since it has no freedom in the moral sense, its actions cannot be called morally "good" or morally "bad," "right" or "wrong."

The situation is very different for persons. For them it is not simply a question of remaining what they are or simply experiencing change without choice. Doing what comes naturally is not enough, even if it were possible just to relax and simply *be*. Rather, persons are faced with the constant necessity of making choices and, in doing so, of determining themselves. How to use their freedom of self-determination—how, in other words, to *be persons*—is the challenge which continually confronts them.

Becoming a person is not the problem

The challenge of being a person is, however, by no means the same thing as becoming a person. Persons *are* persons; the question for them is how to be what they already are. If the problem were how to *become* a person, it would mean that "personhood" was some sort of definite goal or objective toward which one could work by action at the second level. But this is clearly not the case. We already possess personhood. We are not working toward the goal of becoming persons; we are instead coping constantly with the difficult but fascinating problem of how to *be persons*.

Of course it is true that one can become a better person or a worse one. But this is something entirely different from becoming a person. When we say that the question facing us is how to become better persons (or to avoid becoming worse persons) we are saying in effect that the fundamental problem we all face is how to be persons. Questions of better and worse, good and bad, are questions of how.

Thus personhood is not something we achieve, as if it could be the objective of second-level action. The self-made man is a myth, and a confusing one. The question of how to be a person is never settled once and for all in any man's life. It is the basic question with which every man wrestles every day, and all the days, of his life.

The problem is how to be a person

It requires no effort for a person to remain a person. He cannot do anything else. Nor does a person face the challenge of becoming a person. He cannot very well become what he already is.

But for a person the problem of *how to be what he is* is an engrossing challenge. It is a constant question. It is also a lifelong task. The responsibility cannot be evaded. It involves the continual necessity of making choices. One thing about which we have no choice is the absolute imperative of choosing.

Someone might object that suicide offers one way of evading the responsibility of choosing how we will be persons. But this is not the case at all. Suicide is merely one way of responding to the challenge to be a person. Even if one looks at suicide as a kind of choosing-not-to-choose, as an attempt to return to the uncomplicated existence of that which just *is,* it still remains true that this attempt itself is a choice. (Of course, this is true only of suicide when it is freely chosen; if suicide results from insanity, then it is not a free choice, and neither is it a "human" action in the sense of being an action that registers on the moral scale.)

How to be a person is a problem of self-determination. Basically it is a problem which we resolve for ourselves by our choices at the third level of action. It is sometimes supposed that in choosing to do something we are only determining our action, not ourselves. This is not true. When we act at the third level—something we all must do at some point in our lives—we are not just determining our action; we are determining ourselves. In a real sense we are choosing how we will be persons. We are taking ourselves in hand and shaping ourselves through the exercise of our freedom of self-determination.

As we have seen, actions are of three kinds. At the first level are those whose meaning comes from the natural consummation to which they lead. If the action is performed, it naturally ends in this particular result. We do not give the action its meaning—the meaning is already there. When we act only at this level, we are not doing anything that an animal or a small child could not do. We are not determining ourselves; we are simply remaining the sort of thing we already are.

This is not to suggest, however, that a person can simply act instinctively—at the first and simplest level of action—and thereby absolve himself of moral responsibliity. As we have seen, all actions, including those at the third level, can be broken down into their units, and these units are actions at the first level. But these simple units of action do have moral significance when they are, as it were, the building blocks—or the concrete embodiment—of action at a higher level. Thus a decision always to act instinctively would itself have moral significance which would color all the actions performed on the basis of this decision.

At the second level of action we act in order to achieve specific, limited goals separate and distinct from the action. The meaning of the action is derived from its objective. A farmer plants seed in order to grow a crop; the planting of the seed gets its meaning from the harvesting of the crop. A student studies hard simply in order to pass an examination; passing the exam gives meaning to the studying.

We are not determining ourselves by acting at this level either. The meaning of the action is derived from its objective. The objective is outside of us. Even if it is something very important to the person performing the action—and it often is—it is external to him, it is not his *self*. Action at this second level therefore does not involve self-determination.

If, however, a man chose exclusively or almost exclusively to act at this second level, he would in fact be determining the whole cast of his life in a certain way. And this would be a sign of a fundamental commitment, a real act of self-determination, which itself would be a third-level action serving as a sort of umbrella for many actions at the second level. Like actions at the first level, actions at this second level also derive their moral significance from their relation to purposes that go beyond the limited objectives of the second-level actions themselves.

Self-determination

Self-determination occurs at the third level of action. At this level it is no longer a question of action which takes its meaning from the consummation to which it naturally leads; nor is it a question of action whose meaning comes from the specific, definite, limited objective at which it aims. Instead, at this level the meaning of the action is derived from the purpose or good in which one intends to participate by performing the action. It is at this level that the problem and the opportunity of being fully a human person exist.

Notice that at this level of action we speak of "participating" in a good, not of "achieving" a good. When we speak of achieving something, we are speaking of a limited, definite objective which we can, in effect, grasp and possess as a result of our activity. When we speak of participating in a good, however, we are implying that we never fully realize or exhaust it; we are also implying that this participation is not something which occurs only at the end of our activity, and as a result of it, but rather that this participation takes place all the time we are performing the action.

Technique and precise calculation are possible at the second level of action, where we are concerned with achieving specific objectives, but they are not possible at the third level of action, where it is a question of participating in goods. For example, technique and calculation are appropriate and necessary for playing a particular game; one needs strategy in order to win. But there is no way of calculating how to participate in the good of play, how to make playing the game a worthwhile experience for oneself.

In third-level action the goal is indefinite and always extends beyond what is done to achieve participation in it. At the second level of action one can calculate what and how much to study in order to pass a certain examination, but on the third level of action it is nonsense to suppose that one can study just so much and then consider his education completed.

Self-determination is possible only when precise calculation is not. That is to say, it is possible only at the third level of action. When we act in this way we are truly determining ourselves because we are choosing the purposes which constitute ourselves. As we shall see later, the fundamental human goods involved in third-level action are in fact aspects of the human personality; thus we form our characters by the choices we make at this level.

Character might be defined as the residue of self-determined action. When one chooses at this level of action, this is how he *is* until he changes his mind. The orientation given to one's life remains until it is changed. And it can be changed only by a new act of self-determination. This is why even small actions, if they are third-level ones, are important to character formation. When an action involves self-determination, it contributes to the formation of character, whether it is small or large.

This in turn suggests why ethical theories that say individual actions are not important in ethical terms—but only the overall orientation of one's life—are mistaken. Individual actions do constitute the self if they are third-level actions involving self-determination. Even very "small" acts of self-determination are important.

This analysis also points to the inadequacy of the theory that says the morality of actions is determined by the situation. The word "situation" is ambiguous, since it can refer to two different things. One is a set of physical facts—what one might call the "physical situation"—which the individual has not brought about and which is not morally defined since it is open to a variety of possible actions, good and bad.

The other might be called the "moral situation"—the situation created when a particular person encounters a particular physical situation (and in which, presumably, one course of action is objectively better than another). This moral situation is not determined by the physical facts but rather by what the individual brings with him to the physical situation in the way of preconceptions and prior moral commitments.

An example will help to make this clear. The time is sunrise. The place is a downtown street near the railroad station. Lying in the gutter unconscious is a well-dressed man of middle age. This is the physical situation. The moral situation only comes into being when some other individual enters on the scene and is required to make a choice regarding the action he will take.

Let us imagine three different people confronting this physical situation and making a choice about what to do: first, a busy commuter rushing to catch a train which will take him to work; second, a dedicated member of Alcoholics Anonymous; third, a common thief. It is entirely likely that each will respond differently: the commuter by passing by, the Alcoholics Anonymous member by stopping to help, the thief by robbing the man. Furthermore, it is entirely possible that each will feel in his own way morally justified in the course of action he has chosen. Even thieves, after all, are capable of rationalizing their behavior in order to justify themselves in their own eyes—to say nothing of people who are "too busy to get involved."

The point of this example, however, is not to demonstrate that any course of action is acceptable behavior provided one can find some subjective rationalization for it. Quite the contrary. There is little doubt that, in the example given, only the second course of action—stopping to help the fallen man—is, objectively speaking, the morally right thing to do. But that is not the point either.

The point instead is that each of these three persons—the commuter, the Alcoholics Anonymous member, and the thief—encounters the same physical situation but creates for himself a different moral situation because of his preexisting attitudes and commitments. It might be said, for example, that the thief's basic "moral" commitment (which is a highly immoral one) is to thievery. But because this is so, he simply does not see the physical facts—an unconscious man lying in the street—the same way as someone with a different moral commitment. Rather, he perceives this physical situation as one more opportunity for the exercise of his basic commitment to thievery.

In short, the physical situation does not determine the moral situation for an individual. Instead the moral situation is only brought into being by the perceptions and the precommitments of the individual himself. Each person creates his own moral situations—although certainly not the physical situations—on the basis of his own self-determination.

Last of all, it is appropriate to note here that life has more meaning for us when we see the good which is involved in our present situation and perform the action for the sake of participating in that good. Some actions which are, from one point of view, merely second-level actions can, by a change of intention, become actions at the third level. Consider the example of studying. At the second level one studies in order to pass an exam; at the third level he studies, say, in order to learn for the sake of learning itself.

A person acting at the second level is always looking to the future—to the objective he hopes to achieve by his action. But a person acting at the third level is living meaningfully in the present—he is already participating in a good through the action he is now performing. When one thinks about it, there is a certain absurdity in always acting at the second level—always acting for the sake of some objective yet to be achieved. This robs life of its present meaning—because the meaning is always something yet to come, never something now present in which one is at this moment participating.

This is not of course the same as saying that one should always make the best of any bad situation. Indeed, there are some situations one should bend every effort to change. But we are talking about deriving the most meaning from one's present action, whatever it may be. Action has more meaning—more content, one might say—when it is action at the third level.

Just as habitually acting at the third level gives more meaning to life, so it also gives more meaning to death. A man who habitually acts at the third level, the level of self-determination, has participated in human goods throughout the course of his life. His life has been a meaningful one, no matter at what point it happens to end. By contrast, the life of a man who habitually acts at the second level will be deprived of meaning to the extent that death finds him—as it inevitably does—with objectives yet to be achieved.

This analysis of action helps us to grasp better wherein self-determination really lies. Self-determination is a matter, not of achieving specific, limited goals, but rather of participating in fundamental human goods. Next we shall turn our attention to the question of happiness—examining first some inadequate notions of happiness, which correspond to the first and second levels of action, and then seeking in chapter four to determine what happiness really means for a human person. We shall see that what happiness really means corresponds to action at the third level.

Questions for review and discussion

1. What is the difference between "person" as we used the word here and "personality" as we talk about it in psychology or in everyday conversation?

2. How does the idea of "person" held by someone who thinks the fundamental problem of life is how to remain or how to become a person differ from the idea of "person" developed in this chapter?

3. To engage in sexual intercourse as a pair of animals do is an action at the first level; to engage in it as a prostitute does is an action at the second level; to engage in it as a deeply loving married couple does, simply to express and celebrate their love of each other, is an action at the third level. Give other examples of actions at different levels, including, if you can, cases in which the outward behavior remains the same.

4. The three levels of action correspond to the three senses of freedom distinguished in chapter one. Why aren't there distinct levels of action corresponding to political freedom and to ideal freedom?

5. When people in our culture think and talk about action, do you believe they usually have in mind second-level or third-level action? What difference to one's view of life as a whole does it make which of these two levels of action is his customary "model" of action?

6. If third-level action is really determinative of the self, what do the characteristics of this kind of action—for example, the impossibility of calculation—indicate about the sort of reality a person is?

7. Environment is to the organism as situation is to the person. Does an oak tree have the same environment as the cow which is grazing under it?

8. Do you think fictional characters are related to their fictional

situations in the same way that real persons are related to their situations?

9. The three levels of action are related to time in different ways. The motto of the first level might be "Live for the present." The motto of the second level might be "Invest in your future." How is the third level of action related to time?

10. Sometimes it is possible to change what one is doing from second-level action to action at the third level simply by a change of intention. But is it always easy to do so? And is it always a good idea?

3: What Happiness Isn't

Everyone wants to be happy, but the obstacles to true happiness are formidable. It would be naive to suggest that failure to arrive at a correct intellectual understanding of happiness is the sole obstacle to being happy. (One could, after all, know perfectly well what happiness consists in and yet not be happy.) At the same time, however, it would be just as naive to suppose that an incorrect understanding of happiness cannot help to keep a person from being happy. At the very least a man is more likely to be happy if he has a clear and accurate notion of what happiness is than if he has confused some other experience with the experience of happiness.

Many people's ideas of happiness are dominated by one or the other of two quite different experiences. One is the experience of intense pleasure, something which is inevitably a relatively brief and transitory thing. This experience is felt when one reaches the consummation of a first-level action. The other is the experience of seeking some future objective, working toward it, and finally attaining it. This experience is felt when one has the satisfaction of reaching the objective sought in a second-level action. While either of these experiences can be—and often is—mistaken for happiness, neither, as we shall see, provides a good point of departure for understanding happiness. Each falls short of the happiness we would all like.

The problem with pleasure

One trouble with pleasure is that it is a passing experience. Now we have it, now we don't. Furthermore, our awareness that it is transitory constitutes a fundamental flaw in the experience itself. Passing satisfaction does pass and leaves us unhappy—and we know this will be so. Even while we are enjoying ourselves we are half-aware that this experience will soon be over and that we will then return to our customary state of nonpleasure. Being aware of this, we are also aware that our present enjoyment is not so much happiness itself as it is a momentary distraction that makes it possible for us partially to forget our unhappiness.

Another difficulty with intense pleasure is that it is a value only for a part of ourselves. In saying this we do not mean to suggest that pleasure is to be identified with the "lower," "animal" part of man and happiness with the "higher," "spiritual" part. (We would not accept such a division of man into two parts.) The point, instead, is that pleasure—whenever and however experienced—is limited to our consciousness and does not take into consideration the living whole of a human being.

To take an extreme example which makes this point quite clear, it is at least conceivable that a man could derive a great deal of pleasure from eating poisoned food—and die as a result of doing so. However pleasurable his state of consciousness might have been while he was eating the food, we can hardly conclude that the experience was overall a good one for him. This is scarcely what we mean when we speak of happiness.

Yet another problem about pleasure is that we never have it by itself. It always comes riding on the back of some other experience. There is no such thing as an experience of pure pleasure—that is, pleasure and nothing else. And when we reflect upon an enjoyable experience in order, as it were, to isolate the pleasure and enjoy it by itself, we find that the very effort to focus on ourselves in this way undermines the enjoyable continuation of the action which caused us pleasure in the first place. The harder we try to enjoy ourselves and the more we think about it, the more we find we are defeating ourselves in our effort at enjoyment.

An illustration out of the realm of science fiction dramatizes the problem with pleasure and makes it clear why pleasure does not fulfill a reasonable expectation of what it means to be happy.

Suppose it were possible to keep a human brain alive in a laboratory and feed it a continuous stream of artificial brain waves in order to give it the experience of a constantly pleasurable life. Would this be worth doing? Hardly. There would simply be no point in creating a merely pleasurable state of consciousness, apart from real experience and action in a real world. Even if the thing could be done, it would be meaningless, would make no sense. No one would say that the pleasure-experiencing brain was "happy."

This points to the conclusion that states of consciousness, even pleasurable ones, have no meaning and no value in themselves apart from the life which they mirror. A state of consciousness only has meaning in relation to the life of which it is a consciousness. If there were really no lived life (as would be the case of the brain in the laboratory) the state of consciousness would be meaningless.

For purposes of ethics, then, it simply confuses matters

to talk about pleasure, as a state of consciousness, as if it were some kind of norm for human action. Happiness provides such a norm. But pleasure is incapable of doing so. Pleasure pertains to action at the first level. The meaning of life cannot be reduced to this level.

Happiness isn't looking ahead

Other thinkers who have sought to understand the meaning of happiness have taken as their starting point the experience described earlier: of identifying some future goal, working to achieve it, and at last attaining it. This approach locates the ultimate meaning of life in the outcome of action at the second level. St. Augustine interpreted the Christian promise of heavenly beatitude in light of the experience of working toward achieving an objective. Today many people who no longer believe in God, heaven, or hell still identify happiness with the pursuit of future objectives and seek their happiness in this experience.

Nevertheless, the notion of happiness as future satisfaction is not really satisfactory either. This sort of "happiness," which lies always in the future but is never fully experienced now, does not fulfill our expectations of what genuine happiness should be.

Several considerations make this clear. One problem in identifying happiness with the pursuit of future objectives is simply that the objectives are future, and a man who lives exclusively for the future has to a significant degree robbed the present of meaning. When we live in this way, we are in effect making the present a mere means to an ulterior end, whatever the end may be. In this view of things the present has no value in itself; its value comes only from what it contributes to—or takes away from—the achievement of the objective we have set for ourselves. A life lived in this way is a life half lived.

Take the case of a man whose whole life was devoted to

the goal of climbing Mount Everest. For years he has been in rigorous training, scaling lesser peaks, developing his skills, organizing his expedition, and planning his assault on the final objective. At last the time comes. He and his party set off up the slopes of Everest. Halfway up, the mountain climber falls off a ledge and is killed. Everest remains unclimbed.

One's natural reaction to such a story is that the tragic accident rendered the mountain climber's whole life empty and meaningless. His life was built around scaling Mount Everest; he never achieved his objective; therefore his failure to achieve it has robbed his life of significance. But is this really the case?

Isn't it possible that the accident which cut short his life actually spotlighted a glaring fact about his life: namely, that it was empty and meaningless all along? How, after all, could reaching the peak of Mount Everest have given retrospective significance to everything that had gone before? Either there was meaning there all along—or there never was any meaning.

And if his death, short of his goal, makes us conclude that his life was without meaning, this must be because there was never any meaning there. The meaning of a man's life—if any—exists here and now. Making its meaning hinge on something in the future is tantamount to draining it of meaning.

There is another, even more fundamental difficulty in identifying happiness with the pursuit of future objectives. It is that, as far as we know, there is no finally satisfactory state. If happiness lies somewhere ahead, then—at least in our experience—happiness is never reached, for once we reach one objective we simply move on to something else. It is a universal human experience that no one goal gives lasting satisfaction. At the instant we possess one thing, we begin to crave something else. If this is happiness, then happiness must consist in the frustrating experience of never being really satisfied but always seeking something more, something beyond what we already have.

A theologian in the tradition of St. Augustine might reply that this is an accurate enough description of this life, but that this life is not all. The experience of lasting satisfaction, he would say, is something always denied us in this world but enjoyed after death, in eternal union with God.

Even theologically this is not an acceptable position. For such a theologian also holds that God does nothing useless. But if eternal union with God is all that counts, what use does human existence prior to that union have? Either it has none (in which case God *has* done something useless in causing it to be) or it has value in itself—which the theologian in the tradition of St. Augustine is not prepared to concede.

Thomas Aquinas, incidentally, resolves the problem by explaining that the value of our present life lies in the fact that in it we share in God's causing of the future, and in doing so we are more like him than if we shared only in his happiness without living through the process of attaining it.

In any case, to say that our present life derives meaning only from some experience after this life is beside the point as far as ethics is concerned. Ethics is concerned with this life. The question is whether—and how—happiness can be experienced here and now. It is whether—and how—actions which we perform at the present time can also make us happy at the present time. As human beings we live from moment to moment. Our lives are made up of these passing moments and never stand still. To say that happiness in some real sense cannot somehow be found and experienced in the unique, passing moments of our lives is to say in effect that human life is meaningless.

The problem of happiness, then, comes down to this: How can we be happy continually and how can we be happy now? Happiness cannot be mere pleasure because pleasure is a sometime thing; even as we experience it, it slips away from us—and we have all had the experience of feeling pleasure while knowing in our hearts that we are not really happy.

Nor can happiness lie in attaining future objectives. When we have reached one, we immediately begin to crave another. Happiness thus is always deferred, always in the future—and never now. But we live our lives now, not in the future, and *now* is where we must find the meaning of our lives.

To put our conclusion in terms of levels of action: neither the pleasure that arises from first-level action nor the sense of satisfaction that arises from the success of second-level action is adequate to give meaning to human life. We must look toward happiness as a fullness of life corresponding to third-level action.

Questions for review and discussion

1. Although "pleasure," "joy," "satisfaction," and "happiness" are closely related in meaning, they have diverse connotations. Explore the differences, beginning by thinking of cases which exemplify the special sense of each word.

2. Our argument against identifying pleasure with happiness rests on the premise that pleasure is limited to consciousness and consciousness is not all there is to a human being. If personality is equated with consciousness, what is left out?

3. Does someone engaging in an act for sheer pleasure tend to identify himself with his consciousness alone? Compare this with an act in which one engages with another person or persons and in which real communication occurs.

4. There is a conflict in our culture at present between middle-class ideals of achievement and success and the demand for instant gratification. Discuss this conflict in terms of the ideas of happiness developed in this chapter.

5. Marxism condemns religion as the opium of the people—"pie

in the sky when you die." At the same time it argues that the present generation must be sacrificed for the sake of bringing about a future perfect society. Are these positions consistent?

6. Much education is future-directed—organized as a preparation for later life. Discuss the demand for relevance in education in light of this chapter's criticism of identifying happiness with future objectives.

7. Why is it that no one goal we reach in life gives lasting satisfaction?

8. If you knew that you were going to die—in one year, one month, one day, or one hour—what difference would that knowledge make to you? Does your answer tell you anything about the way in which you find meaning in life at present?

4: Happiness Is Being a Complete Person

What is happiness? In the preceding chapter we have examined two possible answers and found them wanting. Happiness, we concluded, is not the same thing as the fleeting and episodic experience of intense pleasure. Nor is happiness identified with the quest for future, always deferred, objectives.

But in seeing what happiness is not, we have also gotten some insight into what happiness is. Happiness must be something which can be experienced in a continuing way (as pleasure is not) and which can also be experienced here and now in each unique moment of our lives (as future objectives are not). The experience of true happiness should be present and continuing.

Obviously this is more easily said than done. This general notion of the experience of happiness does not tell us very much about how to have the experience. So the question to examine now is the crucial one: How?

A whole life

Aristotle developed a theory of happiness which avoided the mistake of identifying it either with pleasure or with the pursuit of specific, future objectives. For Aristotle happiness is a whole life in which man's peculiar capacity, his ability to reason, is realized both in theoretical knowledge and in rationally guided action.

There is much truth in Aristotle's analysis of happiness, but it is not the whole truth. He was correct in locating happiness in the whole life (rather than in isolated episodes or in future expectations). However, he neglected to consider two other important pieces of the puzzle: the role of self-determination and the fact that other human capacities besides reason also make their own unique, irreducible contributions to the experience of happiness.

Aristotle looked at man from a particular perspective and concluded that his peculiar excellence—that which distinguishes him from every other kind of being in our natural experience—is his reason. But if we consider man as a being who constitutes himself through his own self-determination—that is, if we consider him as a person—it is obvious that other areas of life are equally necessary to the fullness of the person. A person is not a disembodied intellect; a person engages in other kinds of activity besides intellectual activity, and these other spheres of experience also make their special contributions to our personhood.

Of course, if we could identify ourselves exclusively with the ideal of rationality, then self-realization and self-fulfillment would lie exclusively in rational activity. The same is true of other purposes and ideals—aesthetic experience, play, even the day-to-day activities necessary for physical survival and well-being. All of these are valid, necessary areas of human activity and experience, and all offer opportunities for self-realization to the extent that they involve and express our freedom of self-determination.

But none of them encompasses the whole of human life and experience. Each is essential, and each, from its own special point of view, is supreme. But no one of them sums up in itself what it means to be a person. To be a person one must respect the unique demands made by each.

We see then that it is not enough to say that happiness lies in the use of reason. This is true—happiness does lie in the use of reason; but it also lies in the use of our human faculties for physical survival and well-being, for play, and for aesthetic experience. All of these are aspects of a human being.

In creating ourselves as persons through self-determination we must act in a way that takes all of these spheres of life and experience into account. We must avoid neglecting or violating the values involved in any one of these areas of life, because they are particular aspects of what it means to be a person, and action contrary to any one involves an assault not on a mere abstraction but on an aspect of our own personhood. In a true sense this would be a kind of self-mutilation.

By contrast, to be happy will, as Aristotle suggested, mean living a whole life. In order to do this one must take a comprehensive view of what human life is. It is not limited merely to one area of human capability. It embraces instead all aspects of the person.

While it is certainly true that no one man can realize to the full what it means to be a person in all areas of life (for that matter, no one man can realize to the full what it means to be a person in one limited area of life), it is equally true that acting contrary to the values inherent in any of the fundamental spheres of life makes it impossible to lead a whole life and thus renders true happiness impossible. To be happy, we must remain open to all of our possibilities as persons.

The question of commitment

Mere openness, however, is not enough. Being a person is not something passive; it involves self-determination. Choices are necessary. We must settle for ourselves the issue of how to be the persons that we are.

Self-determination is only possible when calculation is not. Calculation is a necessary part of human life, but it does not enter into the action of self-determination. Calculation is employed when we seek to achieve specific, definite objectives. A man wants to buy a car; therefore he calculates what is necessary to achieve the objective (how to raise the money, how to select a dealer, how to pick out a car, etc.) and performs the required steps in sequence. His calculations may or may not be correct, and, depending on their correctness, he will or will not achieve his objective.

But the process of calculation is a comparatively simple matter (even though mistakes can be made) because the only question that need be answered about a particular action is whether it contributes to achieving the goal. In other words, the various alternatives can be measured by a common denominator—their effectiveness in reaching the objective. They are accepted or rejected, on the basis of calculation, by how they stack up in relation to the common denominator.

Self-determination, however, is possible—and necessary—in situations where there is no common denominator against which to weigh and measure alternatives. In such situations each alternative is valid in its own way and in its own frame of reference. One could choose any one of the alternatives and not be wrong. For in a situation like this one is not simply making a choice of appropriate means to a limited, well-defined end. One is instead choosing among various purposes which underlie the whole structure of personhood. In choosing in this way—choosing one purpose rather than another—we really choose the purposes which will constitute ourselves. We choose the kind of person we will be.

These acts of self-determination can extend very far; they can in fact control and shape our lives for an indefinite future. An act of this kind is "commitment" in a strict sense.

Such commitment occurs when the act involved has a cumulative aspect, and yet there is no definite end to the accumulation of the particular good. Within such a very large act of commitment there will undoubtedly be a nested sequence of lesser actions which are consistent with and partially fulfill the overarching commitment. Yet no one of these acts by itself totally fulfills the commitment, and in fact all of these acts together do not exhaust the commitment, which is essentially open-ended and always capable of being realized further.

Friendship is an example of such a commitment. In a friendship there is no point at which one can say, in effect, "So much and no more. I have now fully achieved this friendship and need do nothing more about it." One can of course break off the friendship—but then one is ending the commitment. As long as the commitment—and the friendship—endure, there is no point at which one has finally achieved the friendship and can stop acting in ways that fulfill the commitment.

The life of scholarship provides another example. As long as a person is committed to such a life, he goes on accumulating more knowledge without ever being able to feel that he has finally achieved scholarship and can now stop learning. If he does decide to stop accumulating knowledge, he is in effect deciding to withdraw from his commitment to a life of scholarship.

Marriage provides one of the very best examples of commitment. People often say jokingly—or not so jokingly—of marriage, "I didn't realize what I was getting into." Joking aside, however, they are entirely right. No one does know what he is getting into when he makes such a commitment, for the simple but profound reason that it is absolutely impossible to foresee (that is, to calculate) all the actions that will be required in living out and living up to the commitment. No one can know what, in practical terms, the experience will be until he has gone through it.

In such large, open-ended commitments we never know quite what we are doing when we begin. Only gradually, through experience, do we come to understand the meaning of the commitment. And only gradually do we work out in practice the implications of the self we have constituted by making the initial commitment. What we are to be does not exist at the time the commitment is made; what we are to be is what we *become* through individual actions performed under the umbrella of the fundamental commitment.

There are, in short, two aspects to self-determination within the framework of a commitment. What we are to be depends on the one hand on our commitment to a purpose which transcends us and, on the other, to the creative working out of the implications of that initial commitment in the circumstances of life which we encounter.

One other thing needs to be said here about calculation. Calculation is definitely possible within a commitment. In fact, it is not merely possible, it is highly advisable, to use calculation and technique in order to achieve particular objectives which are consistent with the commitment one has made. Merely acting on the basis of impulse and emotion—rather than rationality—does not give a more human character to activity, nor is it more likely to be an apt way of realizing one's commitments in practice.

An impulsive gift, for example, is not the best expression of friendship. Rather, a gift that represents the giver's well-considered judgment as to what is most likely to please and benefit his friend is the gift that will best realize friendship in practice. What is important here, however, is that the calculation be directed toward an objective which is itself directed toward participation in and realization of some good. One is not calculating what gift to give simply to keep one's budget in balance; the purpose of the calculation is instead to determine what gift that can be obtained within one's budget will best realize and express our commitment to friendship with our friend.

How self-determination works

Actions in and by which we truly constitute ourselves have a number of special characteristics. We have already seen what some of these are, but it will be worthwhile to list them here in order to get a clearer understanding of self-determination. Among the characteristics of such actions, then, are the following:

1) When acting in this way we cannot calculate what behavior will be appropriate for our purpose. As we have seen, calculation comes into play—quite appropriately—in seeking specific, well-defined objectives outside ourselves. But when it is a question of determining ourselves, technique and calculation will not do the job.

2) We cannot act efficiently in carrying out our commitments. There is, for instance, no efficient way to fulfill one's commitment to a friendship or a marriage. One can and should of course act efficiently in seeking objectives that are consistent with and help to realize one's basic commitments. But these objectives do not sum up the whole of the commitment, which serves as a sort of overarching umbrella under which many specific goals are embraced and many individual actions performed.

3) We cannot force anyone else, or be forced ourselves, to act in this way. Of course it is possible to force somebody else to perform an action, but by definition an action

one is literally forced to perform by external pressure is not really an act of self-determination. This is not an argument for never forcing people to do certain things or not to do other things: small children should be compelled to brush their teeth, potential suicides should be restrained from jumping out of windows. The point, however, is that no one can be forced to determine himself; he can only do that for himself.

4) In many cases, when we are doing something that we *have* to do, we can personalize it—make it an act of self-determination—by reflecting upon it and consciously locating and choosing a purpose in it to which we are or can be committed. One can, for instance, study simply in order to pass a course—period. Or, one can study in order to pass a course in order to get a degree which will make it possible for one to pursue a profession to which he is truly committed. Or, one can study just for the sake of increasing one's knowledge (with passing the course a kind of desirable by-product). In the latter two cases the act of studying has become more personally meaningful, because it now relates to a commitment which expresses one's self-determination. We can frequently make the necessary events of our lives more meaningful in this way. This is not to say one should not try to change unsatisfactory conditions in his life and in society that can and should be changed. It is only to point out a way of deriving the most meaning from parts of life that cannot or should not be changed.

5) Outward behavior by itself cannot decisively establish whether or not one is acting through commitment. To go back to the example of studying, it is clear that the student studying simply to pass a course could *look* the same and could perform the same external actions as the student who is studying because he loves learning for its own sake. The difference between them is not in their outward behavior but in their intentions.

These five characteristics have one thing in common, and it is this: all illustrate the fact that self-determining action for a purpose intrinsic to the action is quite different from action which is determined by its orientation to an extrinsic goal. However much alike such actions may look from the outside, they are in fact radically different on the inside.

In determining ourselves through our commitments we shape our lives. We establish our way of looking at things. We determine the meaning of the experiences we will have. Thus, as we have seen earlier, we really create situations in a moral sense, because we give the events of our lives and the facts of the world the unique meaning that they have *for us*. This is of course in sharp contradiction to the argument of so-called "situation ethics," which implies that the meaning of a situation is something given, over which we have no control and which we can only passively accept.

How then are we complete persons? This will be the case if our commitments meet certain criteria (which we shall discuss later), if they all fit together to form a harmonious whole, and if we live our lives out in accord with such a harmonious set of commitments. Then we shall be complete persons. And this is what happiness is.

Yet it is clear that as persons living in social relationships with other persons our completeness is not something that comes about in isolation from others. Other people play a crucial role in our being the persons we are. In the following chapter we shall look at some of the implications of this fact.

Questions for review and discussion

1. Explain how Aristotle's notion of happiness resembles but is also significantly different from the one presented here.

2. What are some possible reasons why Aristotle overlooked the capacity of self-determination as central to the human person?

3. What implications might the difference between Aristotle's position and ours have as far as issues involving "mere life" are concerned—for instance, the question of capital punishment or the question of euthanasia for the senile or insane?

4. "Choice" has two senses, corresponding to the second and third levels of action. Distinguish these two senses from each other.

5. Make a diagram representing the relationship between the subordinate ends, intermediate ends, and a final goal in second-level action. Make a different diagram expressing the relationship between subordinate acts and the overarching commitment in third-level action.

6. To what extent can expressions such as "subjective" and "objective," "fixed" and "indeterminate," apply to diverse aspects of a commitment?

7. Why (in terms of the analysis of commitment in this chapter) do newly married couples often begin to experience difficulties as soon as the honeymoon ends?

8. Some people talk about an "art of living" as if there were an applied science (such as psychology) which would be able to give us directions for living a good life. If the position developed in this chapter is correct, can there be an "art of living" in this sense? Leaving aside what is said in this chapter, what arguments can you think of for or against the possibility of devising an art of living?

9. We cannot force anyone else to make a commitment, nor can we be forced ourselves. How, then, can people have any effect at all on each other's commitments?

10. Sociologists dealing with topics involving religion often experience serious difficulty finding objective criteria by which to measure how "religious" different people are. Why do you think this is so?

11. It may be impossible to tell apart the outward behavior of a person acting for an extrinsic goal and that of another person committed to doing what he is doing for its own sake. But if you know two people well, it is likely that you will see certain signs of their true attitude. Apart from what they say if asked, what might such signs include?

5: Persons Complete
One Another

"No man is an island," John Donne wrote. For better or worse (sometimes better, sometimes worse) each of us is linked to many other people by an intricate network of social relationships. Sociologists, political scientists, and other specialists make this obvious fact of human life an object of constant study and analysis. For the student of ethics, too, it raises one of the great and lasting issues in the field—the conflict between egoism and altruism. What sorts of relationships are possible between individual persons? And what moral significance do these various relationships have?

For some philosophers man is primarily a self-seeking individual. In this view society is an artificial creation—a framework for the operation of individual selfishness, an arena within which the powerful can exploit the weak. Other philosophers take a radically different point of view and hold that the community is the central reality. For them individual personality is only a sort of abstraction. Here we shall take the position that neither of these extremes is correct and that the truth about human relationships is situated in a middle ground.

Others as objects

Not all human relationships are the same. The relationship between two strangers sitting side by side on a bus is not the same as the relationship between a husband and wife. Nor is the relationship between either of these pairs the same as that between a bank teller and a holdup man who has just delivered the ultimatum: "Hand over the money, or else!" But it is not saying a great deal simply to state that these relationships are "not the same." We must look closer in order to see where the basic differences lie.

In many human relationships people treat each other as objects. This has a grim ring to it, and in fact the consequences of this way of regarding other people can be extremely grim, leading to such ghastly aberrations as the Nazis' extermination of helpless prisoners in their concentration camps. Yet for all that, this others-as-objects approach is not necessarily immoral. Sometimes it is entirely appropriate.

For example, an engineer seeking to determine the capacity of an elevator sets the limit at a certain number of passengers, based not on their peculiarly personal characteristics but simply on the average weight of the bodies to be carried. It would not help the engineer—indeed, it might make his task impossible—if he had to take into consideration the personalities of the unique individuals who would actually ride in the elevator.

There are also other human relationships which are somewhat more complex and intimate, involving a degree of recognition of human potentiality, but which still do not constitute genuine community. In ordinary circumstances, two strangers sharing a bus seat do not, and need not, enter into a relationship of community; but each does need to recognize the other's human needs and rights at least to the extent of allowing him enough room to sit comfortably.

Many formal contractual relationships are basically of the same kind. The parties to the contract do not need to share common interests, commitments, and points of view beyond the very limited area needed to make the arrangement, whatever it may be, work. And the arrangement works when the objectives which drew the parties together in the first place are achieved.

However, such arrangements do not always work. One bus rider can take up more than his fair share of the seat. One party to a contract can manipulate the terms of the agreement, or violate them, in a way that injures another party or parties. In such cases, where the advantage of the relationship is tipped all in one direction, the others-as-objects approach becomes exploitative and unjust.

No doubt it is already clear from this analysis that this sort of relationship, in which other persons are viewed and treated as objects, is appropriate to action at the second level—action, that is, which is directed to achieving some specific, extrinsic goal. Some human relationships, however, are based not on the seeking of particular limited objectives but on mutual commitment to the same value or values. The relationship in such a case is what we will call "community."

In a community, whether very large or very small, individuals continue to perform their individual, separate, third-level actions—basic, self-determined acts of commitment and also the acts by which they express and realize their commitment in concrete situations. In a real sense, however, there is more here than just the sum total of all the actions of the individual community members. When two or more people unite for the joint realization of a basic good to which they are committed, the community itself is constituted by the common social act which is more than the individual actions of the community members.

The members of a genuine community truly overcome their individual isolation since, understanding and endorsing each other's commitment, they become the common agents of a single action. Of course, each community member may well act differently, doing what is appropriate to his own special role in the community; but at the same time the unity of meaning, the shared commitment, underlying these different actions flows into a single action, in whose performance the community members become one.

It is not necessary for each member of the community to engage in all of the community's behavior. What is necessary is that his behavior be appropriate to his role in the community, that it embody his working-out of the commitment which he shares with all the other members of the community.

Not all members of a baseball team, for instance, do the same thing. The pitcher has one job to do, the center fielder another. However, in playing his special role on the team each makes his contribution to the realization of the commitment which brought the team together in the first place and continues to hold it together.

A baseball team, however, is a very simple example of community. Many communities are far larger and more complex. A nation is also a community, and in the United States the Preamble to the Constitution is the verbal expression of the common action constituting the community. It is an attempt to state in words the values—and the commitment to realize those values—shared by the members of this national community.

The example of the nation as a form of community underlines the complexity of this whole question. For instance, the individuals who originally participated in the formation of the particular community called the "United States" are long since dead. Yet the same social act continues to exist today with new individuals participating in it.

It is also obvious that much more is needed for true community than simply a shared commitment to a value or set of values. As we have seen, it is also necessary that the individual community members act, in ways appropriate to their positions in the community, in order to realize the values to which they are committed.

Furthermore, in a very large community, such as a nation, there is need for an extremely complicated intermediate structure—laws, institutions—between the joint social act constituting the community and the multitude of individual acts performed by the community members as they work to realize their shared commitment. The alternative to such a rational, intermediate structure is, in large communities, chaos.

Another obvious fact about large communities such as nations is that it is not realistic to think of them simply in terms of third-level action. To be sure, the third-level action is the heart of genuine community: there is a basic commitment to some fundamental human value or values, coupled with a determination to realize the value or values through concrete action in concrete circumstances.

But at the same time the real-life fact of the matter is that human communities are never all that pure. One always finds within them a considerable admixture of second-level action: action, that is, which is directed not to participation in some basic human good but rather to the achieving of limited, specific objectives.

This is not a criticism of communities. Individuals often do, and must, act for limited goals; and so do, and must, communities if they are to survive. The important thing, for both individuals and communities, is that the specific objectives and the means chosen to achieve them be shaped by, or at least not in contradiction to, the basic human values to which the individual or the community is committed through self-determination. What makes the admixture of second-level action lessen the communal character of communities is that it is often directed to individual objectives that violate the common purposes of the community as such.

Individual, society, and societies

Most people act most of the time as officials. This may sound like a surprising statement but it is evidently true, provided one understands "official" to mean anyone who is acting in his capacity as a member of a community. To put the matter another way, most of what each one of us does is done as an expression of his role in one community or another. All of us belong to many different communities, and we are constantly acting as members of them.

Consider some communities to which the average person may belong: the community called "the family"; the community called "marriage"; the community called "the company"; the community called "the church"; the community called "the nation"; the community called "the university"; communities called "the team," "the club," "the gang," "the neighborhood," "my best friendship," and so on. One could go on and on. Any individual, upon reflection, can put together an extremely long list of communities to which he belongs—and will probably overlook some in the process.

The point is that each of us has not just a few social roles but many different ones, depending on which particular society is in question at a given time. And in the normal course of events almost everything we do is done by virtue of our membership in one or another of these societies. It is a tendency of human action to be communal and social in nature.

We belong to some societies because we have chosen to belong. We belong to others without really having made an explicit choice. Most people, for example, become citizens of a particular nation, and therefore members of that particular national community, by an accident of birth, not as a result of their own deliberate choice.

In many ways this is a practical convenience, but it can also present grave difficulties for an individual. By reason of his membership in a particular community he can become involved in a communal act without any decision on his own part, and perhaps without even knowing of it (as may happen, for instance, in the case of infants and children who are involved in the actions of the various communities into which they have been born). Difficulties arise for the individual when one of the communities to which he belongs undertakes a communal action with which he cannot conscientiously agree. If, for instance, one's country becomes involved in a war which one regards as unjust, one faces some very hard choices imposed by membership in that national community.

An individual's role in society consists of the various things that he can do—and some of which he is obliged to do—in virtue of his participation in the society. The role is not a catalog of things the individual actually does; it can rather be thought of as a list of things he can do and (in some cases) should do because of the position he occupies in the community.

A society or community depends for its existence on the fulfillment of their roles by its individual members. In a sense, therefore, each member of the society is dependent on every other member. It is of course true that an individual can fail to perform some of the requirements of his role without destroying the social act and, thereby, the society. A marriage can continue to exist even if one or both partners are something less than punctilious in carrying out their respective marital roles. A nation can continue to exist even if some citizens neglect some or all duties of citizenship.

At the same time, however, there is in every society a certain minimal level of role fulfillment, varying with the society, which is essential if it is going to continue to be. If a significant number of the members of a society (the significant number will be different for different societies) fall below this level, the community will simply disintegrate.

We have already seen that every individual belongs to many different societies and as a result has a number of different social roles. This can very well raise problems for the individual as far as his self-determination is involved. Briefly put, the heart of the problem lies in selecting one's communities in a way that makes one's life a unified whole. If one's membership in one society requires a commitment and forms of behavior which are in conflict with the commitment and behavior demanded by membership in another society, something will have to give. Ordinarily, one cannot be a functioning member of both the community called "marriage" and a community of hermits; it is difficult to belong to the society known as the peace movement and the society known as the armed forces.

These are extreme examples, but more subtle and complicated ones often crop up in the lives of individuals. Indeed, in times like ours when individuals ordinarily enjoy many different opportunities and options—to belong or not to belong to many different societies—the problem of harmonizing social roles and avoiding conflicts of duty can be a very serious one. The best solution to the problem lies in prevention: in looking ahead, assessing the duties that membership in a particular society will involve, comparing these with the duties involved in membership in other societies so as to foresee conflicts, and opting in or out of communities according to one's judgment as to whether the social roles involved will or will not be in conflict.

This is much better done before the fact. Opting out of a community to which one already belongs generally involves far more pain and dislocation, for oneself and the other members of the community, then electing not to join the community—when one has the option—in the first place.

Authority

This analysis of societies should help to shed some light on what is today a rather sensitive issue: the role of authority.

In second-level relationships (situations involving specific means to well-defined objectives) "authority" is virtually synonymous with "power." Authority in such relationships is involved only when one person sets down requirements and another person or persons are obliged to fulfill them. The person exercising authority here is simply exercising managerial power and no more than that.

The situation is, however, quite different in cases of true community, where a third-level social act (a commitment to a shared value or values and to actions expressive of this value system) is involved. The role of authority here is to articulate the common, overall social act and to plan the organization of behavior by members of the community so as to realize its purposes. Authority in such a situation is not an inherently bad thing; on the contrary, it is simply necessary. Furthermore, it is a form of service to the community rather than a way of exercising power over the community.

In real life, though, authority does become a problem because of the mixed nature of many societies. They are not wholly third level or wholly second level but something of both. As a result, the role of the authority is similarly mixed: a combination of service and power. This, too, is neither good nor bad—it is just a fact of life. But it does open the door to abuses.

On the side of authority the obvious abuse is to emphasize power over service, and sometimes to exercise power while pretending it is service. This is the accepted style of dictators and tyrants, both large and small, who present themselves as "protectors of the common interest" and as "servants of the people" while they in fact dominate and exploit the people whom they profess to serve.

However, the problem does not lie exclusively on the side of authority. The other members of the community also can abuse the relationship. This comes about in the case of the individual or group which seeks to enjoy a free ride—taking advantage of the benefits to be derived from belonging to the community while avoiding the contribution to the community required by his or its social role. It is a temptation, one frequently succumbed to, for an individual in this position to attack authority for being "exploitative." Doing so, after all, gives the free-loader a measure of ostensible justification for failing to carry his fair share of the burden of making the community work.

No one person can actively pursue, much less realize, all the purposes for which human beings can strive. Life is short, the abilities of any one person are limited, and in committing oneself to strive to realize some purposes one inevitably gives up the possibility that he will also seek actively to strive for others.

In a real sense, however, community compensates for our individual limitations by making possible the realization, or at least an attempt at the realization, of valid, important human purposes which any one of us, singly, is incapable of realizing. United in community, persons are able to respond to the demands of all the goods for active service.

Community, common commitment, thus does not always take the form of our actively working together. More fundamentally, it means that each member of the community recognizes and respects the human goods to which other members of the community are dedicated. Often this will express itself in appreciation of the particular interests and ways of life of others, and in satisfaction at their accomplishments. Altruism lies at the heart of community: a sense that it is more important that the good be realized than that we, as individuals, realize it ourselves.

Some people deny that genuine love of others is possible. It would not be possible if it meant that we had to seek an alien good, a good which was foreign to us and in which we felt we had no part. It is possible for us to love each other, however, if we are committed to seeking together a good or goods which we feel to be our own and yet recognize to be "bigger than both of us."

Others deny the significance of the individual and of his unique responsibility, since they see him as all but obliterated in society. But genuine community does not come about by denying our individuality, our otherness, in a blind effort to submerge ourselves in an anthill society. Community is based instead on a shared commitment in which each individual shoulders his special share of the responsibility for realizing the values which originally drew separate persons into the relationship we call "community."

We have up to this point learned something about the meaning of freedom, about the various kinds of action, and in particular about the kind of action which is self-determination. We have considered happiness, which is closely tied to freedom of self-determination. And we have looked at the crucial role of social relationships. All this, however, has only laid the groundwork for determining what makes action morally good or bad. It is time now to begin to consider this central question. Our first step will be to examine and criticize views that would make it impossible to say for sure what is right and what is wrong.

Questions for review and discussion

1. One theory of society is the organic view, which sees the individual as hardly more than an abstraction from the social whole. This is sometimes called "the anthill society." Do you know of any specific theories of this sort, or any historical attempts to bring into reality societies which conform to such a model?

2. Large corporations (and other organizations) spend a great deal of money on personnel offices and public relations staffs to try to personalize their relationships with employees and customers. In what circumstances and to what extent can such efforts be genuine?

3. In a true community what unites the members into a single whole? What distinguishes them so that they do not get lost in that whole?

4. Some people fear loving and being loved because they are afraid of losing their identity in too close a relationship. Do you think such a fear can be well grounded? If so, how can the problem be overcome?

5. Analyze the Preamble to the U.S. Constitution as an example of a community-forming act. Compare this with mutually exchanged wedding vows as another example of a community-forming act.

6. Can the same society simultaneously involve aspects of genuine community, of contractual relation, and of exploitation? Why would it be important to take account of these various forms of relationship in order to understand the behavior of people in a society?

7. Compare the problem of integrating his social roles faced by a modern man with the problem faced by a member of a primitive tribe.

8. Some ethical theories give a very special place to the political community, going so far as to hold that ordinary ethics does not apply to it. According to the theory presented here, the political community is only one among others and not exempt from the claims of ordinary ethics. Why is this so?

9. Find and discuss concrete examples to illustrate the different

meanings of authority and the ambivalence present in relationships involving authority.

10. Community is impossible among people who do not think that there is anything bigger than both (or all) of us. Does this "something bigger" necessarily imply that there is some superhuman reality, such as God?

6: We Don't Always Know
What Is Good for Us

We are free to choose what we will do. But we are not free to make whatever we choose right.

We must follow our best judgment concerning what we ought to do. But our best judgment can be mistaken.

For many people these four statements are simple and unassailable. For many others they are neither—indeed, they are flatly untrue. These statements contradict various forms of relativism and subjectivism which are extremely prevalent today and which, for the beginner at least, constitute a major obstacle to serious reflection regarding ethical issues.

What is meant here by "relativism and subjectivism"? Although the words do not commonly come up in conversation, the attitudes they stand for are commonplace. How often, for example, when it is a question of whether a particular action is right or wrong, has one heard it said, "It all depends on what the society you live in regards as good" or, "It all depends on the kind of life you want to live"? Shorthand expressions like these sum up a whole approach (at least, a conscious approach) to ethical problems: "It all depends. . . ."

Of course, in a certain sense it all *does* depend. Decisions about the right and wrong of actions depend on many different factors, including those so strongly emphasized by cultural relativism and individualistic subjectivism. As with many other approaches to ethical questions, relativism and subjectivism are not totally devoid of truth. The trouble is that they have fastened upon particular truths and, in doing so, have excluded other aspects of reality which must be taken into consideration in developing a well-rounded ethics which respects the facts of human experience. They are not totally divorced from reality; rather they are distortions—distortions because they single out certain aspects of reality and ignore others.

Relativism and subjectivism make ethics (that is, the serious and sustained examination of one's life and society from the viewpoint of what actions should and should not be performed) a virtual impossibility. It is true that they can properly be described as ethical theories, but they are ethical theories which cut short the ethical enterprise. They deny in principle that moral judgments can be simply true or false.

If this were so, the effort to examine one's life or one's society by methods of rational criticism would be ultimately pointless, since the conclusion of any such examination would always be "It all depends on the kind of life you want to live" or "It all depends on what the society you live in regards as good." Inevitably this marks a rather conclusive dead end to any reasoned effort to decide what actions are right and what actions are wrong, and why.

It should be apparent by now that the position we are taking is reflected in the series of propositions at the start of this chapter. "We are free to choose what we will do. But we are not free to make whatever we choose right. We must follow our best judgment concerning what we ought to do. But our best judgment can be mistaken." It is not enough simply to assert these things, however. In order to hold and develop these positions it is necessary first to get over the hurdle proposed by relativism and subjectivism. This is what we shall now undertake to do.

Cultural relativism

Cultural relativism is an offspring of anthropology, the study of the customs and beliefs of other cultures. Although cultural relativism is rejected by many contemporary anthropologists, it continues to have an impact on popular attitudes.

Everyone has encountered cultural relativism at one time or another. The conversation turns to some exotic practice—human sacrifice perhaps—and invariably the cultural relativist in the crowd will say something like, "Well, if these people really believed (or believe) that it was the right thing to do, no doubt it was right *for them*." He is expressing the view that norms of right and wrong action are totally derived from the society in which one lives; there is no other criterion of right and wrong than what one's own society happens to believe on the matter, since in the last analysis all such norms are determined by social conditioning and by the circumstances and needs of particular cultures.

Upon reflection most people instinctively draw back from wholehearted acceptance of cultural relativism, since they do not really care to be put in the position of saying that such things as human sacrifice or cannibalism or ritual prostitution are good and proper if only society happens to regard them as such. However, there are better reasons for rejecting cultural relativism than the instinctive repugnance people feel for the conclusions to which it logically leads (even though that instinctive repugnance is itself not without significance in the matter).

For one thing, as we have noted, cultural relativism is

now losing support even in the professional anthropological circles in which it once prevailed. It is perfectly true that there are striking differences between the ethical values of particular cultures. But these differences are to a great extent explicable in view of differences in physical conditions, beliefs, knowledge and ignorance, levels of scientific and technical progress, and other accidents of history prevailing at different times in different societies.

More fundamentally, contemporary anthropology has pierced beyond the surface of the differences which distinguish one culture from another and succeeded in identifying the basic points of convergence in which superficially very different cultures are in fact very much alike. Cultures have come to be seen as various ways in which human beings seek to satisfy common, underlying human needs. These needs correspond, as far as the testimony of contemporary anthropology can tell us, to certain basic, universal human goods.

Consider an example. Life is one basic good—a value respected, so far as the evidence shows, at all times in all cultures. This is not to say that all cultures have expressed their sensitivity to and respect for life in the same way. On the contrary, very primitive tribal cultures limit their respect for life to members of the tribe, the group, those who are identified—by whatever criteria—as belonging to "us."

In other cultures respect for the value of life is extended to embrace others who are not identifiably part of the small ingroup, until, ideally, respect for human life is extended to all those who possess life (a point at which, possibly, no culture in history has yet really arrived, and which certainly is still beyond contemporary culture). In spite of the extreme diversity, however, centering basically on the question of who are and are not members of the group whose lives are deemed deserving of respect, the important fact is that every culture in some way manifests awareness of and respect for the value of life.

The same is true of many other basic human goods: the begetting and raising of children which has always been recognized as a central value by every culture; intellectual knowledge; play or recreation; and so on. The particular ways in which recognition of these values has been expressed by different cultures have varied enormously. But running as permanent threads through all cultures has been recognition that such values are important and indeed fundamental to human life. Thus the problem with cultural relativism is that it represents too superficial an analysis: one which, in emphasizing the differences among cultures, fails to take into account the basic samenesses below the surface.

Apart from these considerations, cultural relativism has become increasingly irrelevant in our times for the simple reason that culture, as it has been historically understood and studied by anthropology, is disappearing. There is today perhaps no truly isolated group left in the world—no group that has been unaffected by the beliefs and attitudes of other groups—and if there should be such a group, it seems certain to vanish in the near future as a result of the impact of communications technology.

Our world appears indeed to be moving toward the day, perhaps not too far in the distance, when it will be possible to speak no longer of "cultures" but only of a single "world culture" in which variations of belief and custom will be of relatively minor significance. As this occurs, it becomes increasingly artificial to attempt to apply the concept of cultural relativism to the realities of life.

Finally, as a practical matter, it should be noted that if one were to be consistent in espousing cultural relativism, one would logically have to apply this theory to one's own culture. Doing so would make it impossible to criticize the values of the society in which we now live. If ethical values are endowed with validity simply by the fact that a culture accepts them, then there is no ground on which a person can criticize or reasonably seek to change the values of his own society.

The effect of this is to make impossible any effort to achieve reasoned social change; instead social change comes to depend on the ability of individuals and groups to impose their will, their vision of how things ought to be, on other individuals and groups in society.

Individualistic subjectivism

Even more prevalent, perhaps, than cultural relativism is the attitude known as individualistic subjectivism. It is based on the belief that each individual spins his own moral norms out of his own interior and that, ultimately, the only criterion by which to judge behavior, one's own or someone else's, is consistency. The only judgment possible is that one either is or is not living according to the standards he has set for himself. "It all depends on the kind of life you want to live."

Obviously, if this position is correct, it makes no sense to argue either for or against any moral proposition about which different people disagree. There is really no standard according to which one can maintain that, say, the dropping of the atomic bomb on the civilian population of Hiroshima was wrong, or, for that matter, that it was right. Assuming the people who made and executed the decision were doing what they thought they should do, one can only agree that undoubtedly what they did was the right thing to do.

Yet it is equally obvious that people do attempt to argue for and against such moral propositions, almost as if they intuitively recognized that there are moral norms which transcend the limits of individual preference and consistency and apply to many (perhaps all) men. In practice, no one concedes that differences about fundamental moral issues are on the same level as differences of taste concerning such things as music and painting.

If subjectivism were correct, it would mean that in the end no one could ever do anything really wrong, except through lack of sophistication. We are after all free to choose what we will do; and if that freedom can make what we choose right, who would ever choose to do anything while choosing at the same time to make it wrong?

It might be objected that, in this view of things, "inconsistency" (not living up to one's subjective standards of behavior) is "immorality," and that it is quite possible for a person to be inconsistent, and therefore immoral, as a result of confusion or inconstancy. But one can easily enough be consistent without being constant, provided he is ingenious enough to incorporate so many qualifications and limitations into his moral decisions that no one decision is ever really binding, as a matter of consistency, in the future. All that "consistency" in this sense requires is enough sophistication to arrange things so that inconsistency becomes a practical impossibility.

In any case, a closer look at subjectivism discloses that the whole theory is built on ambiguity and confusion in the use of language. Subjectivism comes down to this: whatever a person decides is right, is right for him. But the word "decide" is being used here to refer to two very different things: judgment and choice. We decide (judge) what is right, and we also decide (choose) what we will do. But the two kinds of deciding are not the same, and subjectivism goes wrong in ignoring this fact.

Likewise, it is necessary to make a distinction between the rightness or wrongness of what we do and our individual guilt or innocence in deciding to do it. It is possible to commit atrocities with a good heart, just as it is possible to do good deeds with evil intentions. In the first case the goodness of the intention has no effect on the badness of the deed; just as in the second the goodness of the deed has no effect on the badness of the intention. The intention and the action are and remain separate, and each must be considered in making judgments about the morality of one's own or other people's action.

If, finally, subjectivism were correct, we could not help knowing what is morally right for us to do. Yet that which is morally right for us, whatever it may be, must surely be that which is, in the moral sphere, most profoundly good for us as persons. Our common experience, however, tells us that we do not always know what is really good for us in other areas of life: in matters affecting our health, for example, or our vocational choice.

If it is frequently so difficult for us to know what is best for us in other areas of life, why assume that it should be so simple in the moral sphere—so simple, indeed, that whatever we choose is automatically the best thing for us? None of our attitudes in other areas of life is beyond rational examination and criticism. Why suppose that it is different in the moral domain?

If, then, it is not true to say that we make whatever we choose right by the fact of having chosen it, it is clear that we stand in need of standards to apply in making our choices—standards by which we can determine whether the things we choose are right and also whether our reasons for choosing them are right. In the chapters that follow we shall see what these standards are.

Questions for review and discussion

1. Why are relativism and subjectivism in principle incompatible with the position that ethical judgments can be simply true or false?

2. Are white South Africans members of a different culture from

that of black South Africans; from that of white Americans; from that of black Americans?

3. The truth underlying cultural relativism is that, as a matter of fact, there are wide differences between the ethical values of particular cultures. Why doesn't this fact settle the ethical issue in favor of relativism?

4. Some cultural relativists used to criticize members of Western societies for their intolerance of the primitive ways of less civilized groups. Do you see any incompatibility between offering such criticism and holding the theory of cultural relativism?

5. Why is an affirmation of freedom of self-determination compatible with the denial of subjectivism?

6. Distinguish between subjectivism and the position which says that each person is obliged to do what he or she sincerely believes to be right (the obligation to follow one's conscience).

7. If subjectivism were correct, would it make sense to say that an individual is "guiltless when he does what he sincerely believes is right, even though he happens through no fault of his own to be mistaken in this belief"?

8. As a matter of fact, more people are likely to express a subjectivist attitude on questions of sexual morality than on questions of social justice, such as racial discrimination. Again, some people who were absolutely certain that the Vietnam war was immoral hold a subjectivist position on such issues as the morality of the use of drugs. Do such differences necessarily mark inconsistencies? How can such differences be explained?

9. Rejecting relativism and subjectivism doesn't mean that one must hold that all people in all places at all times have exactly the same moral obligations. Can you think of reasons why—even though moral judgments are objectively true or false—different people should have different moral obligations?

7: Purposes - Ulterior and Otherwise

If subjectivism and cultural relativism are not adequate guides in the difficult task of judging human action—our own and others'—we must look elsewhere for such assistance. The search is not easy. But an examination of the purposes for which people act is an important step in the right direction.

A note about terminology is important at the start. The purposes we will be discussing can just as well be called "goods." In this context, however, use of the word "goods" does not mean that we have reached the stage of being able to discriminate between what is *morally* good and bad. That is yet to come. At this point we are only using the word "good" to refer to a possible purpose of third-level action, whether it be morally good or bad.

Also, the purposes or goods we will be discussing here are very broad in scope—so much so, in fact, that it is difficult to find a single label which adequately describes any one category. The friendly reader is asked to be sympathetic and to understand that the labels we will use are attempts at identification rather than precise definition.

Purposes

Everyone is familiar with the expression "ulterior motive." When we say that a person has an ulterior motive, we mean that the purpose for which he is acting is not being sought for its own sake but as a means to something else. There is nothing unusual or inherently wrong about this. People commonly act in this way, and there is no reason to criticize a workman, say, who does his job not exclusively or even mainly for its own sake but in order to earn what he needs to support himself and his family.

At the same time, however, there are purposes which can be sought not as means to an end but for their own sake, without reference to anything else. Unless he has extraordinary presence of mind, a drowning man struggling to keep his head above water is simply striving to stay alive and has nothing else in view except that. Unless he is unusually calculating, a child absorbed in piecing together a jigsaw puzzle is simply working the puzzle for its own sake, not in order to please his parents or to improve his mind. Unless he is unusually insensitive, a man listening to a beautiful or stirring piece of music is enjoying the music for its own sake, not because he has bought a concert ticket and wants to get his money's worth.

These simple examples illustrate the fact that there are purposes or goods for which one can act for their own sake, without reference to any other purpose. It is in such purposes that one participates by third-level action. On closer examination it appears that they fall into several broad categories.

One group of purposes can be lumped together under the heading "life." Certainly this category includes the preservation of life—so-called "matters of life or death."

But it also includes various aspects of life, such as health, safety and the avoidance or removal of pain. Also encompassed here is procreation, the begetting of new life and the rearing of children; for a couple can desire to have a child for no other reason than that they want to have a child.

A second group of purposes can be labeled "play." This category includes games and sports, all the things one normally thinks of as play, but it also includes a great deal more besides. It is possible for a person to engage in extremely taxing and strenuous activity, physical or mental, and still be playing, even though a casual observer might be disposed to call what he was doing work. One is in a play situation whenever he engages in a performance simply because he enjoys the performance itself. If he does it just because he likes it, the next man who swims the English Channel or goes over Niagara Falls in a barrel will be playing.

A third group of purposes which can be sought for their own sake lies in the area of "aesthetic experience." This includes not only such things as enjoying works of art—music and paintings, for example—but other, superficially very different experiences. The pleasure one takes from contemplating a beautiful scene in nature can be an aesthetic experience. So can the pleasure one takes from watching a football game on television. Obviously there are specific differences between a football game and a ballet, and yet watching either can involve a genuine aesthetic experience. An aesthetic experience is one which a person seeks because he values the experience itself, not because it leads to anything beyond itself. Unlike play, aesthetic experience involves, not action of one's own, but rather the internal experiencing of something which comes from the outside.

Yet another group of purposes can be labeled "speculative knowledge." As one might expect, speculative knowledge is knowledge which is sought for its own sake, not because it is useful as a means to some other end. It is, quite simply, knowledge sought to satisfy curiosity. Because "speculative knowledge" has a rather formidable ring to it, one might tend to identify it solely with the activity of such apparently detached thinkers as philosophers and physicists. Yet the quest for speculative knowledge is often involved in much more down-to-earth situations—in such things as the activity of the child who takes a clock apart to see how it works, or of the housewife chatting across the back fence with a friend about the new family which has moved into the neighborhood.

While the purposes grouped in these four categories are obviously quite different from one another—and indeed, as we shall see, cannot be reduced to one another or to some common denominator which underlies them all—they do all have at least this much in common: it is possible to understand them without reference to the action of an agent seeking to realize them. As purposes, their meaning exists independent of human action (which is not to say that they themselves have an independent existence, as if they were Platonic Ideas). For this reason it is convenient to group them all together under the heading "substantive purposes."

There is, however, another group of purposes which can be sought for their own sake but whose meaning inherently implies human action. Self-determination is involved in their very meaning. Furthermore, since third-level action is involved both in what the purpose is and in one's participation in it, one can label this group "reflexive."

Every person experiences tensions within himself. The contemporary concern with getting-it-all-together points to the fact that people generally sense that they are *not* able to get it all together—at least not permanently or to the degree that they wish. Different aspects of the self seem continually to be at war with one another, and the human response is to struggle—more or less successfully for different individuals at different times in their lives—to resolve these tensions and conflicts and achieve inner harmony. The objective being sought is integration of the various aspects of the self. And the purpose here is quite appropriately referred to as "integrity."

A similar tension exists between the inner self of the individual and his external action. It is true that an action is the act of the person performing it, and yet the action is something other than the actor. Conflict is possible here, too, a conflict expressed in such comments as "I wasn't really myself when I did that" or "If I had known then what I know now, I wouldn't have done it."

Such conflict is also reflected in our comments on other people, such as the damning criticism that someone is a phony. What we are expressing in such cases is a judgment that an action (or actions) is not consistent with the inner attitudes of the person performing the action; there is a lack of harmony between what the person is and what he does. The effort to close this gap and achieve this harmony—between ourselves and our lives—is also directed to a fundamental purpose. This purpose we call "authenticity."

Looking further beyond the self, it is apparent that we experience tensions in our relationships with others, and we also seek in many ways to overcome these tensions and establish harmony between ourselves and other people. The purpose sought is "friendship." In using this word it is necessary to note that it has a very broad meaning here. In popular parlance friendship is used only to describe the relationship of persons who are close to one another. As a basic purpose or good, however, friendship encompasses many other things—for example, justice and peace among individuals and groups, even the harmonious relationship between entire nations. In this extended sense one could say that, ideally, friendship is the fundamental purpose of an organization like the United Nations.

Finally, in this group of reflexive purposes one moves beyond even the relationships among people to consider the relationship between human beings and God. It may be objected that we are now entering the realm of theology or that we are attempting to assume the existence of God. That, however, is not the intention. We do not presume at the moment either to demonstrate or to take for granted that God exists.

What is significant here is simply the fact that—whether or not God exists—men in all cultures and at all times have been concerned about their relationship with a transcendent *Other* to whom the name "God" is usually given. This concern has focused either on the attempt to re-establish a harmonious relationship with the Other (a relationship believed or felt to have been disrupted in some way) or to strengthen and perfect this relationship where it exists. This category of purposes can be labeled "religion," and the various things done by various men in various cultures in the attempt to restore harmony between themselves and the transcendent Other (however understood) are all directed to religious goods.

At this point the question very legitimately arises, Is this all? Does this list of four substantive purposes (life, play, aesthetic experience, and speculative knowledge) and four reflexive ones (integrity, authenticity, friendship, and religion) exhaust the categories of purposes which can be sought for their own sake? It seems so.

Anyone, of course, can identify many more purposes than these, purposes which to particular individuals or particular cultures seem or have seemed far more important than any of the ones listed here. But upon examination it becomes apparent that other purposes are actually no more than aspects or combinations of aspects of these fundamental purposes. The fact that they may seem more important to an individual or a group simply reflects the cultural conditioning or psychological leaning of that individual or group.

Historically, for example, particular societies have placed their major emphasis on such goods as patriotism and have made it their supreme purpose. Yet "patriotism"—a word describing the relationship of mutual loyalty and support of individuals in the same country—is no more than a limited aspect of the broader category we have called "friendship."

Again, an individual person may say that the basic goal of his life—the purpose which gives everything else meaning—is some such good as self-fulfillment. But "self-fulfillment" is a blanket term which will mean different things to different people but which in any case will be made up of various aspects of the goods we have described here.

In short, these eight purposes seem to be all of the fundamental purposes of human action. Any other purpose either will include a bit of some or all of them or will represent a limited aspect of some of them.

Are all purposes equal? Yes, but . . .

But while other purposes are reducible, in one way or another, to the purposes we have been describing here, these eight purposes are not reducible to one another, nor can they be reduced to a common denominator—some ultrafundamental, bedrock purpose which underlies all the rest. It would make matters much simpler if there were a common denominator, for in that case whenever one was confronted with the necessity of making a choice, one could simply determine on the basis of calculation which available option best realized the common denominator purpose in this particular situation and then act accordingly.

As a matter of fact (and complexity), however, each of these eight fundamental purposes is—looked at from its own point of view—the most important. This is one of the things that often makes the choice of action so difficult. Possibly this sounds like a surprising statement. Is there then no hierarchy of values? In a sense there is, but not in the sense that one can rank these eight fundamental purposes in rigid order according to their relative importance.

Every individual has a rough hierarchy of values of his own insofar as some purposes are more important to him than others, but this is a matter of subjective choice and temperament. Obviously, too, we often make the judgment that someone who, say, puts success ahead of honesty (who is willing to cheat and lie to get what he wants) has a false hierarchy of values; but this is based on our working assumption that dishonesty is immoral and that if one has to choose between being moral and being successful, one should choose to be moral.

All this is true enough, but we repeat what we said: there is no objective hierarchy of values among the eight fundamental purposes we have been examining, because each in its own way is most important.

Someone may find this acceptable enough in regard to a purpose like life or religion, but a bit hard to swallow in the case of play. So let us take play and see how it can be called the "most important" value.

From its own point of view, play (as we have described it here—engaging in a performance simply because one enjoys the performance) is the most important thing in life. Most people, after all, spend most of their waking hours working more or less doggedly simply in order to have a little leisure in which they can do what they want to do—in which, in other words, they can play. Further-more, unless people are occasionally able to get away from the necessary side of life and engage in play, no other purposes can fully open up to them.

This is true even in regard to religion. If there is no room for the notion of play—doing something because one likes to do it—in one's approach to religion, and if religion is a matter of strict quid-pro-quo necessity, then one has effectively debased religion by reducing it to a kind of deal with the transcendent (I will sacrifice my oxen in order to please the gods and make the rain fall, etc.). If religion is to be something more than a contractual relationship be-tween oneself and the Other, one has got to leave room for play.

One could run through the rest of the purposes and see that the same is true of all of them. Life is most important because unless a man lives he loses the opportunity to realize any other purposes. Speculative knowledge is most important because unless one has a grasp of truth, he lives a truncated, partial life. Religion is most important be-cause unless one is on satisfactory terms with God (the transcendent) nothing else really matters. And so on. Looked at from its own point of view, each fundamental purpose is most important.

This is not to suggest, however, that these purposes are not related to one another. As a matter of fact, the four reflexive purposes (integrity, authenticity, friendship, and religion) are so intimately related that to the degree one is failing to realize one of them, he is failing to realize them all. This is because each involves, in a different way, the quest for harmony in life—harmony among aspects of the self, harmony between one's self and one's action, har-mony between the individual and other people, and harmony between individuals and the transcendent Other whom we call "God." It is simply a fact of experience that when any one of these relationships is disturbed, the other relationships are also affected and to a degree undermined.

Furthermore, the reflexive purposes are related to the substantive (life, play, aesthetic experience, and speculative knowledge) in the sense that the latter must serve as vehicles for the former. It is impossible to act simply to achieve a reflexive purpose—and no more. Inevitably it is necessary to include some substantive purpose in one's action in order to give content to the activity by which one seeks to realize the reflexive purpose.

Consider friendship. Presumably one seeks to realize friendship by being friendly. But a friendly act must have some substance to it. If a young man and young woman go on a date together (a friendly act), the date has got to involve some sort of specific activity: taking a walk in the park (play), going to a concert or a movie (aesthetic experience), talking (speculative knowledge—with perhaps a bit of play or aesthetic experience thrown in), or whatever.

The reverse, however, is not true. Substantive purposes can be sought by themselves, without reference to reflexive purposes. The drowning man struggling to keep his head above water has just one end in view—saving his life. It is most unlikely that he is concerned at the moment with integrity, authenticity, friendship, or even religion.

In listing and describing these eight fundamental purposes, we do not mean to suggest that they already exist fully or even that, conceptually, they are fully determinate. In a real sense nobody can say precisely what is meant by play, life, integrity, authenticity, and the rest, because they have never been fully realized and never can be.

Why not? Simply because these purposes constitute the outlines of human possibilities—the outlines, in short, of what it means to be a human being. And, as such, just as we cannot help but understand them to some extent (because they are part of us, because they sum up what it means to be what we are: human beings), so we can never fully comprehend what they mean because we never in our lives exhaust the fullness of what it means to be human.

No matter how deeply we explore any or all of these fundamental human purposes, there is always something beyond—some further possibility for realizing, within these eight categories, what human life is all about. The only way in which we can gain ever-deepening understanding of these purposes is by dedicating ourselves to them and seeking their realization in our lives and the lives of others.

Questions for review and discussion

1. Why is working for money not one of the basic purposes listed in this chapter?

2. Many empirical psychologists would list such things as food, drink, oxygen, and so forth as basic needs. How does the position set forth here take into account the fundamental character of activity directed toward satisfying such needs?

3. Traditionally, liberal education has been concerned with play, aesthetic experience, and speculative truth. But as education becomes available to a larger part of a population, it tends to become less liberal and to concentrate more on vocational preparation. Why do you think this is so?

4. Can you develop a theory explaining why an interest in play, aesthetic experience, and speculative knowledge might have developed as mankind moved from more primitive to more civilized conditions?

5. What is the difference between "substantive" and "reflexive" purposes? Can you think of other expressions that would mark this distinction?

6. By what principle are the four kinds of reflexive purposes differentiated from each other?

7. Do you know of any theories in psychology, ethics, or other fields that tend to define the ideal of the good human life in terms of one (or less than all) of the purposes distinguished here?

8. Acts done simply because they are morally virtuous have

traditionally been considered ends in themselves. If this view is correct, the moral virtues must be included in the scheme of basic purposes. Where would they be included?

9. It might be argued that you cannot act for any one of the reflexive goods without to some extent tending to realize all of them. Can you think of reasons for or against such a position?

10. Discuss the problem of the hierarchy of values. In order to set up a definite hierarchy there must be a single, definite principle of ranking. Why can't a principle like self-realization serve as this principle?

11. According to our thesis, reflexive purposes require substantive ones as vehicles. Illustrate this idea by the example of a quest for international justice.

12. Using examples from history, show how one of the purposes—for instance, justice—can be definite enough to serve as an objective but also open-ended enough to permit the unfolding of new dimensions of meaning.

8: "Ought" Points toward Fullness of Being

Having examined the fundamental purposes for which it is possible to act, we have made some progress in the difficult task of establishing guidelines for making moral judgments about action. But we have not yet answered the central question, What makes some actions good and others bad? This basic issue still confronts us.

Curiously enough, though, it is a fact of everyday life that people regularly and without difficulty make value judgments in areas other than morality. They spontaneously say that various objects and experiences are "good" or "bad" and that certain things have been done as they "ought" or "ought not" to have been done. Examining what is meant by such expressions when they are used in nonmoral areas of life will not immediately tell us what they mean when applied to moral questions. It will, however, give us some insights which will help us to understand moral "good," "bad," and "ought."

Good and ought, bad and ought not

The meanings of the words "good" and "ought" (as of the words "bad" and "ought not") are closely related. Their relationship becomes clear when one looks at areas other than morality.

A good car is one which does well what a car ought to do. Of course, different people have different ideas about what a car ought to do, and thus they may disagree on whether a particular car is good or not. One driver puts the emphasis on speed and judges that any car which cannot do 120 mph. is not a good one. Another driver is looking for economy and concludes that only a car which gets twenty miles to the gallon is good. Such differences, however, are beside the point here—the point being that, however an individual determines what a car ought to do, a good car for him will be one which meets his particular standards of oughtness.

The same fact (that "good" is closely related to "ought") is universally observable. A good argument is one which reaches the conclusion an argument ought to reach (although there can certainly be strong differences of opinion about what that is). A good diet is one which provides what a diet ought to provide (a healthy gourmet may see this in quite a different light from an overweight man concerned about his heart condition). A good mother does what a mother ought to do (different mothers certainly have different views on this).

All this simply points to the fact that, while there is plenty of room for disagreement about what a car or a diet or a mother ought to do, everyone who uses the words "good" and "ought" quite naturally understands that they are inseparable in meaning (as are their counterparts "bad" and "ought not"). This is not a moral judgment; we are not even dealing with morality here. It is simply a judgment that the good thing will be the thing which is as it ought to be.

What exactly is this judgment expressing? What do we mean by saying that the good thing is the thing which is as it ought to be? To answer this question it is necessary first to take note of the fact that existing things are often incomplete. Part of their reality is still in the order of potentiality. They are *something,* certainly, but they are not yet everything they can be. They have not yet become all that they are capable of being.

Furthermore, the possibilities of actually existing things are not mere fictions. It is not a fiction to say that a child is capable of becoming an adult. The future adulthood of one's children is a very real thing, even though it does not yet exist. Adulthood for a child is an entirely real possibility which he has simply not yet reached and realized.

We are not, however, leading up to the conclusion that moral goodness means fulfilling one's possibilities, while moral badness is failure to fulfill possibilities. The matter is a good deal more complicated than that. After all, badness is as real a possibility as goodness.

The car which one purchased in the hope and expectation that it would be a good car can turn out to be a lemon, constantly laid up in the shop for repairs. The child whom one raised to be a good person can turn out to be evil, and in so doing he is fulfilling some of his possibilities in as real a way as he would if he were good. A man who is cruel, who exploits others, who breaks down community, realizes his potential to the extent that cruelty, exploitation, and the destruction of community were among the possibilities open to him. The mere realization of a possibility does not mean that a thing or a person is thereby good.

Being and being more

Some theories of what it means to be morally good and morally bad say in effect that goodness is health and vice is disease. This is the explanation offered, for example, by the psychoanalyst Erich Fromm. It is not an adequate explanation, because it does not leave room for freedom of self-determination and, in ruling out this freedom, it rules out the whole moral question as well.

If, after all, vice is simply a form of disease, from which one suffers but which one does not choose, then self-determination just does not enter into the picture; and, as we have seen earlier, activity which is not the result of self-determination is not moral action at all (that is, it is neither moral nor immoral; it is simply amoral). It is true that some men act viciously because they are diseased, but in such cases they are not acting immorally, even though they are acting viciously. Where freedom is lacking, one cannot properly call action either moral or immoral.

While it is not possible to accept the goodness-health—badness-disease theory, the notion does contain the kernel of an idea worth exploring. Both "health" and "disease" describe ways in which an organism can function. How do we distinguish between them? Health, briefly put, is that way of functioning which is compatible with and leads to functioning further and more fully; disease is a way of functioning that interferes with and closes off possible functions.

In the nature of things, a disease makes an organism less capable of functioning; if the disease is serious enough, it eventually makes the organism incapable of functioning at all because it ends in death. Health on the other hand is a condition in which the possibility of functioning is open, and the more healthy the organism is, the more capable of functioning it is. Thus what is good for the organism (health) is to live and live more fully, whereas what is bad (disease) is for it to live less fully and eventually not to live at all.

A similar pattern exists in the area of thought and inquiry. In this field, too, we make value judgments by saying, for example, that a particular argument is "good" or "bad." This need not be a moral judgment at all. One can properly acknowledge a good argument for what one regards as a morally bad position, just as one may recognize a bad argument for something he regards as morally good.

Various criteria enter into the nonmoral judgment that an argument is good or bad. One thing demanded of a good argument is clarity; no one regards confusion as desirable. Another trait is certitude; it is considered desirable that an intellectual inquiry lead to a conclusion instead of losing itself in vague rambling. A third criterion is explanatory power; in natural science it is considered desirably that a hypothesis be able to account for a number of phenomena, rather than that a new hypothesis be introduced to explain each individual phenomenon. Finally, one desires consistency; a train of thought should hang together and its components should not contradict each other.

Why are these characteristics—clarity, certitude, explanatory power, and consistency—regarded as desirable? Because when they are present it is possible for knowledge to continue to grow and expand, and new areas for investigation and further understanding can open up; whereas when they are absent, further growth in knowledge and understanding becomes impossible. Confusion, endless inquiries, the absence of unifying principles, inability to explain things, internal inconsistency—these block thought and terminate investigation. The process by which we acquire further knowledge is halted. Thus, in the area of thought and inquiry the good is that which makes possible further growth in knowledge; the bad is that which frustrates and renders impossible further growth.

The same pattern is repeated in the area of art and technology. Creativity in fine art basically refers to the opening up of new possibilities in a particular medium. The most creative artists, masters like Mozart and Rembrandt, are those who significantly expand the borders of their art form. Lesser artists, on the other hand, are those who for the most part operate within the confines of what has already been achieved in a particular genre; they come up to the mark but they do not exceed it. As for artistic failures and hacks, they do not achieve even what has already been achieved; their efforts fall short of the standards set by their predecessors and thus tend to set art on a retrogressive path.

In technology, too, creativity means the opening up of new possibilities for further development—the sort of thing achieved by an Edison. Efficiency is also regarded as desirable in these areas, and efficiency is good because it fulfills possibilities in a way that leaves open further possibilities. By contrast, stultification sets in when the creative spirit flags and investigators are unable to go beyond what has already been achieved. Inefficiency is likewise bad because it not only fails to set new standards but does not even measure up to old ones—because, in other words, it tends unnecessarily to limit possibilities.

In all of these areas—health, intellectual activity, art and technique—we value or regard as "good" that which leads to being and being more; we judge to be "bad" that which cuts off further possibilities and tends toward the restriction of being.

This is very abstract language, to be sure. But the abstractness is necessary in order to sum up what one observes over and over again in concrete instances in many different areas of life. The good is on the side of that which promotes being and its expansion and fullness. The bad is on the side of that which limits and contracts being and eventually terminates it in nothingness or nonbeing.

What about morality?

We still have not arrived at an understanding of moral good and bad, but we are in the process. Up to now we have simply seen what in various fields, apart from morality, is meant by such words as "good," "bad," and "ought." We have not discovered anything very surprising—only that, in very general terms, the good is that which preserves being and makes possible more being, while the bad is that which limits being and tends toward nonbeing.

It is reasonable to suppose that the same pattern is present in the moral area, with adaptations required by the particular subject matter of morality. The subject matter of morality is free human action.

If what we have just said is correct, then moral goodness will be found in a kind of free human action which not only realizes man's potential for free action but realizes it in a way which tends toward ever-fuller realization. By contrast, moral evil will be a way of acting which also realizes man's potential for action but does so in a way that closes off possibilities for further free, self-determined action.

This is very general indeed and scarcely enables us to determine whether a particular action is morally good or bad. Even at this very general level we must examine more closely what the principle we have just expressed means and why it is plausible to regard it as the principle of moral good and evil. Beyond that, it will be necessary to see how the principle—if it is valid—can be applied to concrete circumstances in order to make moral judgments about individual actions.

Yet the fact remains that, tentatively at least, we now do have a very general principle for discriminating moral good and evil. Moral good is that which fosters human *being* and *being more*, human living and living more fully.

Moral evil is that which puts limits on human *being* and contracts human life.

Moral evil amounts to a kind of existential suicide; moral goodness amounts to ever-increasing growth in the realization of one's possibilities as a human person. But what makes such growth possible? In the next chapter we shall try to answer that question.

Questions for review and discussion

1. Some have argued that "good" is the more basic concept, others that "ought" is more basic. We do not directly enter this argument. Do you see why not?

2. If someone thinks of potentiality as nothing more than a way of referring to actuality at some time in the future, he would not be able to make sense of the theory we are outlining here. Can you think of arguments for or against the position that when we say "X can" we mean something more than "X will, if certain conditions are fulfilled"?

3. Some philosophers say that values are irreducible to facts— "ought" is irreducible to "is"—while others say values are nothing but a particular set of facts. How does the position outlined here resolve this issue?

4. To what field does the concept of "health" belong? Biology? Investigate the history of the concept and current attempts to define it, and compare with our analysis.

5. Good and bad in the area of thought and inquiry are in the province of logic. If you have already studied some logic, analyze what was done in your course with reference to the criteria for this area that we suggest.

6. Exemplify from the field of art and literary criticism the way in which originality is used as a criterion of quality in the fine arts and literature.

7. Compare our remarks about efficiency with definitions of it to be found in introductory works in economics.

8. Some propose self-realization or self-actualization as the moral ideal. This position is obviously related to ours. But for several reasons we avoid such a formulation. How is our formulation more complex?

9. It has been said that the most fundamental question in ethics is, "Who makes the rules?" Criticize this formulation of the problem in light of the analysis proposed here.

10. In each of the fields discussed in this chapter the values involved lead to do's and don't's, and the standards of what ought to be lead to negative evaluations of that which falls short of the standards. Does this mean that disciplines such as hygiene or logic are essentially negative and restrictive? If our analysis is correct, would the same conclusion apply to ethics?

9: Two Ways of Choosing

"To be or not to be." Hamlet stated the problem quite well. Although he obviously had something else in mind, his famous words neatly sum up the two fundamental kinds of choice which are possible: choice in favor of being and choice in favor of nonbeing.

The question of choice is important at this stage of our discussion because it will carry us forward in the task of identifying and understanding more clearly the criterion of moral good and evil. Up to this point we have seen that the very notion of moral good and evil inevitably involves freedom of self-determination. Where there is no freedom, no self-determination, morality is not in question at all.

We have also seen that, in order to be possible, human actions must be for purposes. If there were such a thing as an absolutely purposeless act, it would not be what we mean by a "human" act, which is directed to the realization of some purpose or good.

Thus the criterion of moral good and evil must involve both these elements: freedom and purpose. It will be concerned with self-determined action performed in view of purposes. But this is to say that the question of choice is inevitably involved in the whole matter of establishing a criterion of moral good and evil, for choice is inextricably linked with both freedom (where there is no choice, there is no freedom) and with purposes (where many purposes exist but not all can be realized, one must choose among them).

At this point we should recall something noted earlier about purposes. Fundamental human purposes are not outside us but within us. They are aspects of man, intrinsic human possibilities whose realization is up to us. When a person acts to realize one of these purposes, he is not acting to achieve something outside himself. Rather he is striving to bring into being some part of himself by participating (taking part) in the good toward which he acts.

Realizing fundamental human purposes is not like acquiring material possessions (although in particular cases acquiring possessions—or renouncing them—may be a means to the realization of purposes). Rather, at bottom, it is self-realization, a way of creating oneself by giving reality to aspects of the self which had previously only been possibilities.

In the previous chapter we said that the meaning of the word "ought," when applied to morality, parallels (with due regard to morality's proper subject matter) its meaning in other areas. "Ought" generally points toward full, fuller, and fullest being. The moral "ought" thus points toward full and fuller freedom of self-determination and, ultimately, to the fullest possible self-determination. But since "self-determination" is simply another name for realizing what it means to be a person, "ought" in the moral sphere points ultimately to an ideal of the fullest possible personhood. The moral "ought" is a kind of verbal road sign directing travelers to full humanity realized through freedom of self-determination.

If expressions like "the fullest possible personhood" and "full humanity" sound more than a little vague, there is good reason for it. Everyone has in the back of his head some more or less hazy notion of what "full personhood" means for him. In the nature of things, however, this ideal will always be more or less unclear.

It is possible to set specific objectives for oneself—to become a doctor or a lawyer, say—and then set about achieving them in an efficient manner. But it is far different when it is a question of realizing one's ideal of personhood, which is likely to encompass such things as being wise and loving and religious. Purposes like these are open-ended; in practice a man comes to understand their meaning in his life by working it out for himself through a process of self-realization that extends over a lifetime. There is simply no way of mapping out in advance the steps to be taken in achieving one's fullest possible personhood through the realization of fundamental human purposes.

If there were a way of mapping in advance the steps to be taken in achieving one's fullest possible personhood, that could only be because one's fullest possible personhood was an objective of second-level action. In that case one's fullest possible personhood would be a limited, definite objective extrinsic to oneself—which is absurd. We are dealing here with choices which are true exercises of freedom of self-determination. In such choices, as we have seen, one opens oneself to participation in goods; one does not limit oneself to specific objectives extrinsic to oneself.

Therefore, an individual bent on realizing his personhood must leave himself as open as he can to the fullest possible range of human goods. And this is a question of choice. In making choices—as one must—he must choose in a way that leaves him open to further self-realization. Put negatively, he must as far as possible avoid making choices in a way that cuts him off from goods not chosen and locks him into a narrow and evermore restrictive pattern of personhood. A man must choose in a way that does not obstruct his growth but instead makes self-realization a lifelong process.

Choice—exclusivistic and inclusivistic

We return now to the point at which we began—"to be or not to be." As far as choice is concerned, that sums up the available options: choice which permits further growth and choice which obstructs it.

One way of choosing can be called "exclusive" or, better perhaps, "exclusivistic." It may be objected that all choice is exclusivistic, since in choosing one thing an individual naturally excludes the things not chosen.

While this is certainly the case, it ignores the fact that there are two radically different attitudes which one can bring to choosing. In making a choice among alternatives one can do so in such a way—and with such an attitude—that those things which are not chosen are also not positively rejected, or one's attitude can be such that the alternatives not chosen *are* rejected. The second way of choosing—with an attitude that positively rejects the alternatives not chosen—is exclusivistic choice. Let us take a closer look at what it involves.

It is Sunday morning. You roll out of bed, turn off the alarm clock, and confront a choice: What to do this morning? There is nothing that you *have* to do; whatever you decide to do will be something you could choose for its own sake. There seem to be three possibilities: first, go out and buy the Sunday papers and spend the morning reading them; second, play golf; third, go to church. Having thought the matter over, you decide to go to church. (We are, incidentally, not trying to advocate church-going; the example will work just as well if either of the other options is chosen.)

The question is, Having elected to spend the morning at church, how do you now feel about reading the papers and playing golf? If your choice has been made with an exclusivistic attitude, your state of mind may now be more or less as follows: "Who wants to read the papers anyway? All you get is bad news and ink on your fingers. It's a waste of time. And golf? Knocking a ball around with a stick is an occupation for nitwits. I can't see why anyone would even bother." So off you go to church, with a good conscience but a decidedly exclusivistic attitude.

There are several things to notice here. Before the choice is made, each of the three options—reading the paper, playing golf, and going to church—is perceived to have value. You would find some meaning in doing any one of them. Since it is possible to do only one, however, you must choose among them. And in choosing one your attitude toward the other two undergoes a dramatic change. Abruptly, playing golf and reading the paper, which originally seemed like good, satisfying ways of spending the morning, take on a negative cast. As options not chosen, they have become things to reject and disparage.

It is now not enough to leave them in the category of the not-chosen; it is necessary to cut them down to size by finding fault with them and, quite possibly, distorting the goodness of the option that was chosen (e.g., "Just think of all those sinners playing golf this morning or lying in bed reading the Sunday papers, while I, virtuous soul that I am, am giving glory to God and setting a good example to my fellowmen by going to church"). Before the choice

each of the three options had its own good about it, but
after the choice only one—the option chosen—is still seen
as good, while the other two, subjectively at least, have
been stripped of their goodness and rendered worthless.

The same thing happens whenever one chooses exclusivistically. In doing so a man limits the good to what he
has chosen, while denying the value of that in which he
has elected not to share. He whittles down human possibilities to fit himself and his limitations. Implicitly or
explicitly he asserts not only that what he chooses has
value but that *only* what he chooses has value, and that the
things he does not choose are thereby rendered valueless.
This means that implicitly or explicitly he denies that
values are standing human possibilities, which have value in
themselves, and hence which can keep their value even if
an individual does not choose to act toward them in a
particular choice.

But it is also possible to choose with an inclusive—or,
better, an inclusivistic—attitude. This means simply that
while choosing one alternative out of two or more, one
continues to respect the values present in the alternatives
that were not chosen. A person who chooses in this way in
effect acknowledges his own limitations—no one can be or
do everything—but he does not shift the blame, as it were,
onto the options-not-chosen by denying their value.

We can see more clearly what this means if we return to
our example. Once again the choice is the same: to go to
church instead of reading the papers or playing golf. But
this time the choice has been made in an inclusivistic
manner. What then is one's attitude toward the other two
alternatives?

Quite simply, it will be honest recognition that there is
merit in both of them. Reading the papers is an infor-
mative and entertaining way of spending one's time; playing golf is good exercise and a lot of fun. One has not

chosen to do either on this occasion, but one's appraisal of their value remains exactly what it was before the choice, and this is exactly what it would have been if they had been chosen instead. All the options possess certain values, and the mere fact that one has not chosen two of them is no reflection on either of them, but simply an indication of the fact that nobody can read the papers, play golf, and go to church simultaneously.

We ought always to choose inclusivistically. For consistent inclusivism in choice is in fact the criterion of moral goodness we have been seeking, whereas moral evil consists in choosing exclusivistically. Indeed, it can be said that no one chooses precisely to do *what is morally wrong;* one rather makes choices *in a way* that is morally wrong—in an exclusivistic manner.

This is so because, upon reflection, it becomes apparent that inclusivistic choice corresponds to what we suggested earlier as the meaning of the moral "ought"—the fullest possible realization of ourselves as free. When we choose inclusivistically we remain open to further self-realization even in directions we have not chosen. Even though we have chosen X—instead of Y or Z—we continue to acknowledge the good that is in Y and Z and, in doing so, we remain open to the possibility of realizing that good, given different circumstances. We have not closed off growth in any area of life (which is to say, growth in ourselves).

By contrast, because it involves an attitude which denies the value of that which is not chosen, exclusivistic choice not only prevents self-realization in these directions here and now but tends to block it permanently by creating a mind-set which denies the goodness that is there. If, to return to our example for a moment, one has once persuaded oneself that reading the paper or playing golf is valueless, one has by that very fact made it at least a bit more difficult—and possibly a great deal more difficult—

ever to engage in that activity (and thereby realize the value involved) in the future. One has narrowed the dimensions of his own personhood.

The meaning of immorality

The truth of what has just been said becomes more clear when we see that the criterion of moral evil outlined here fits the various meanings of the word "immorality." When we say that something is immoral, we are saying that it is a kind of self-mutilation, that it represents irrationality in action, that it is a violation (at least incipient) of community, and that it is a rejection of God (or the transcendent Other).

First, self-mutilation. When a man is confronted with a choice, each alternative corresponds to something within him reaching out to be realized. In any choice among alternatives, of course, something goes unrealized. But in exclusivistic choice the aspect of the self which is not realized is suppressed and denied. It is told in effect not only that it cannot be realized here and now but that it should not be realized, because it is not reaching out to any value. When this happens, a part of a man's personality dies a little; if it happens often enough, it may die altogether.

Second, irrationality in action. In order to see the options in a choice situation as real alternatives, one must take for granted that each has some genuine value or goodness. Before the choice is made, one hears the appeal made by the value in each of them. But when a man chooses exclusivistically (acts immorally), he not only declines to respond to the appeal of the alternatives not chosen; he must also refuse to hear it—he must deny that there is anything there to hear. Thus he makes himself deaf to an appeal to which he cannot possibly be deaf—because it comes from within himself. He must deny the reality of that of which he is perhaps all too aware—because it is part of him. To put this point in a more literal and abstract way: one who chooses exclusivistically treats as not-good what is not chosen, but what is not chosen had a *chance* to be chosen only because one had recognized it as a good. Herein lies a kind of inconsistency which is not logical contradiction, but which is irrationality in action.

Third, violation of community. When one chooses exclusivistically, he is in effect saying that the alternatives he has not chosen are without value. If, then, someone else confronted with the same alternatives makes a different choice, it will follow that the second man has chosen what is worthless. And someone who chooses what is worthless is presumably either stupid or perverse. Thus exclusivistic choice inherently creates a situation of conflict between the individual who chooses in this way and others who make different choices; whereas one who chooses inclusivistically, because he continues to recognize the value in what he has not chosen, is also able to acknowledge the reasonableness and decency of others who make different choices from his and to appreciate the enrichment of the human community brought about by the very fact of difference.

Fourth, rejection of God. Immoral action is also called sinful or antireligious. A genuinely religious attitude acknowledges that human purposes and possibilities have meaning which transcends the particular significance they have for the individual, meaning related in some way to the transcendent Other whom we call "God." However, the man who chooses in an exclusivistic manner in effect asserts that the good is simply that which he chooses, and "goodness" means no more than what he causes it to mean by his choices. Inclusivistic choice by contrast leaves one open to the possibility that the meaning of "goodness" and the meaning of one's own life are not limited to whatever arbitrary content one gives them oneself but do in fact derive at least partly from their relation to something or someone transcendent. Exclusivistic choice denies that goods that are not chosen have any higher principle that sustains them as good even when they are not chosen; inclusivistic choice affirms (in an implicit way, usually) the reality of transcendent support for human possibilities.

It bears noting, finally, that inclusivistic choice involves an attitude of service to—rather than domination of—the goods or purposes of human life. The man who chooses in this way is not imposing his vision on reality; rather, he acknowledges goodness where it exists and seeks to realize it to the best of his ability even while admitting that, because of his own limitations, he cannot realize every possible human purpose in his own life. This mode of choice thus corresponds to the third level of action which, as we have seen, basically involves the realization of human goods through participation in them.

If, however, one regards the alternatives in a choice situation in such a way that not choosing something transforms it by removing the value which it previously possessed (exclusivistic choice), from then on one is involved only in action at the second level. For this implies that a thing has goodness only insofar as it is a concrete objective and that, if one chooses not to seek it and to possess it, it ceases to have value.

This is the paradox—the irrationality in action—of exclusivistic choice, seen now from another point of view. One sets out to make a free choice, to exercise self-determination; one ends up pursuing a particular objective, his action now merely a matter of doing as he pleases. Instead of realizing himself by remaining open to fuller personhood, the person choosing exclusivistically makes even that aspect of himself that is fulfilled by his choice into a definite and limited objective, which is now *extrinsic* to the very center of his personhood. Choosing exclusivistically, one moves *from being* a person to *having* something one happens to want.

This is not to say that it is impossible to act immorally at the third level. The point rather is that immoral action at the third level of action in a sense consists in choosing to place oneself at the second level—and stay there. We shall see more of what this means later.

Questions for review and discussion

1. One reason some people take a subjectivist position is that they are afraid of an externally imposed morality—one which would make morally good action into second-level action. Discuss the way in which the theory outlined here reconciles objectivity with freedom.

2. Is inclusivism itself exclusivistic inasmuch as it excludes its opposite?

3. In what sense can one choose to do what is morally wrong?

4. Think of examples of actions which you consider morally evil but in which you can nevertheless find the good for which the action is done.

5. Discuss the difference between self-mutilation and self-restraint. Do you know of any theories of moral development that confuse the two?

6. What is the difference between the rationality in action demanded here and the consistency that even a subjectivist theory requires?

7. Some theories of ethics hold that the morally good is what builds up community, while the morally bad is what harms others. Distinguish the criterion of morality proposed here from such alternative theories.

8. Some religious theories of morality reduce moral goodness to obedience to divine commands. William of Ockham, a fourteenth-century theologian, went so far as to say that if God commanded us to do just the opposite of what the Ten Commandments say, we would be morally obliged to do so. How does our view of immorality as rejection of God differ from religious theories of that sort?

9. The theory proposed here rejects the idea that in choice we create or transform values. How, then, can it be said that in this theory there is room and necessity for creativity in moral life?

10. If immoral action occurs at the third level, it must be directed toward at least a partial and mutilated aspect of one of the eight categories of fundamental human purposes discussed in Chapter 7. In which category do you think the good lies to which immoral acts are directed?

10: The Ethics of Love

Any advocate of the new morality who has followed the discussion up to this point is probably ready to explode by now. "What has all this talk about levels of action, substantive and reflexive goods, inclusivistic and exclusivistic choice got to do with morality? Who ever heard of such hairsplitting? There is no need to make a production out of moral judgment—and all your jargon just obscures what is in reality perfectly simple. The moral criterion is love. If a man acts lovingly, he is acting morally. That's the long and the short of it."

Would that it were so simple! Unfortunately it is not. Several different ethical theories are embraced under the vague headings of the "new morality" or "situation ethics," but none of them provides an adequate account of human action or the standard by which moral judgments are made. And the slogan, "It's all a matter of loving and acting lovingly," turns out upon examination to be no more than a source of confusion at best and, at worst, an excuse for avoiding the hard task of judging—and acting—morally.

Relatives and absolutes

One of the theories encompassed under the heading of the "new morality" or "situationism" is the moral relativism expressed by John Dewey. In this view there are no absolute values; all values are merely relative to a particular situation. The value of values, one might say, is determined by the situation, not by anything inherent in the values themselves.

This is a rather pure version of the situationist ethic. Basically it is founded on a false understanding of the reality of a moral situation. The situationist assumes that, morally speaking, the situation is something given which imposes morality on us.

Actually, however, the reverse is true. The situation does not impose morality on us; we impose morality on the situation. That is to say, the moral dimension becomes present according to the manner in which we perceive the facts of the situation and respond to them through our free, self-determining choices.

We have already made this point earlier, but it is worth returning to it here in the context of our discussion of the new morality, the "love is everything" ethic. To illustrate what we are saying, let us take one of the most sensitive moral issues of our times, the Vietnam war, and the appropriate response of individuals called on to participate in that war.

Leaving aside all passionate rhetoric, there were only two judgments one could make about participation in the war in Vietnam: it was moral or it was immoral. Now let us imagine two draft-eligible young men—John and Steve—faced with induction in 1968, at the height of U.S.

ground involvement in Vietnam. What was the moral "situation" confronting them?

For John the "situation" is this: South Vietnam, a small, peaceful country friendly to the United States, has for all practical purposes been invaded by aggressive, communistic North Vietnam. The United States, prompted by altruism, has gone to the aid of the aggressor's victim. It is a classic case of a Good Samaritan stepping in to protect the weak from being victimized by the strong. John accepts induction into the army willingly, convinced that it is right for him to do so.

For Steve the "situation" is this: two factions of Vietnamese are squabbling for control of their country. The United States, obsessed with anticommunist zealotry and anxious to retain its strategic foothold in Southeast Asia, has intervened on behalf of the military dictatorship which heads one of the factions. Its intervention has been unusually violent, resulting in widespread loss of civilian life. The war is immoral and the U.S. should have no part of it. Steve refuses induction into the army, convinced that it is right for him to do so.

The purpose here is not to argue the morality of the Vietnam war. It is instead to illustrate that the moral "situation" created by the war could (and did) appear very different to different people. And as a result of their different perceptions of the situation, different people responded in very different ways. If situationism were correct, this simply could not have happened; the situation would have forced the response on individuals. But in fact just the opposite happened. Individuals in effect created the moral situation for themselves on the basis of their preconceptions and their understanding of the facts.

A situation, in short, does not impose morality on an individual. Rather, the moral element is determined by the individual's judgment of the situation and the course of action he freely chooses for himself in light of that judgment. To appeal to the situation as a source of moral determination is simply to refuse to reexamine one's moral assumptions. When we say that the morality of a situation is "given" by the situation itself, we are only saying that our preconceptions have caused us to perceive the situation in a certain way and that we are not interested in taking another look—at either our perceptions or our preconceptions—to see whether they square with reality: "Don't confuse me with facts!"

Utilitarianism

Also embraced under "new morality" is the theory of utilitarianism which received its classic statement in the works of Jeremy Bentham and, in particular, John Stuart Mill. Basically, utilitarianism holds that when a choice must be made, the morally right thing to do is to choose the alternative which will result in the greatest net good or (if the alternatives will have adverse consequences) in the smallest net harm.

Bentham equated goodness with pleasure—but this was soon seen to be a faulty explanation because it leads logically to the conclusion that, for example, a happy pig is in a more fortunate condition than Socrates. Mill advanced the theory by arguing that the good involved is the greatest happiness for the greatest number of people and by recognizing further that it is not just the quantity of pleasure or happiness which is important but its quality.

Utilitarianism, however, necessarily involves a number of grave difficulties which render it unacceptable as an ethical theory. For one thing, to suppose that the moral criterion is the greatest good (or happiness) for the greatest number of people is, as Mill correctly recognized, to reduce morality to a matter of quantitative measurement. This in turn demands that there be a common denominator of goodness or happiness; in other words, that all purposes or values be ultimately reducible to the same thing so that they can be measured by the same yardstick.

As we have seen, however, the fundamental human purposes cannot be reduced in this way. Each is the most important purpose from its own perspective and none is reducible to another (nor are all reducible to some overarching superpurpose). Merely quantitative measurement is thus impossible in moral matters.

Furthermore, an exact calculation of the net good and evil consequences of action, as envisioned by utilitarianism, can only be made at the second level of action, where one acts to achieve concrete, limited goals. In effect, the theory seeks to determine the success or failure of action in achieving specific objectives.

But morality, as we have also seen, is basically concerned with self-realization through third-level action (action by which one determines one's self through participation in fundamental human purposes). Calculation of the kind presupposed by utilitarianism is impossible at this level of action because the values or purposes involved are not embodied in a set of specific external objectives to be achieved but are instead aspects of one's own personhood to be realized through the process of self-realization.

Finally, Mill's recognition of qualitative differences among goods or pleasures itself introduces a fatal flaw into utilitarianism, even though at the same time it opens the door to a more accurate understanding of what morality is all about. Mill was quite right in acknowledging that enjoyments (goods, pleasures, purposes) are qualitatively different. But precisely because they are so, it is obvious that there is and can be no common denominator, no universal measuring rod, of the sort which would be imperative for utilitarianism to be a viable ethical system. Thus utilitarianism turns out to be a dead-end street, an illustration from the field of ethics of the futility of trying to add apples and oranges—or, better, of trying to say which is larger: the number 756 or the length of a rainbow.

At bottom, utilitarianism amounts to telling a man to act in order to achieve what is good—without answering the question of what is good. If it assumes that every kind of goodness is fundamentally the same as every other kind, so that all can be weighed on the same scale, it assumes what is untrue. If it acknowledges that there are different kinds of goods which are not reducible to a common denominator, it is correct—but it has also thereby ruled out the kind of calculation about means and ends which alone would make utilitarianism workable.

Love is/isn't everything

Other objections can easily be added to the list of criticisms of utilitarianism-new morality-situation ethics. For instance, what really is the situation in question? The situationist will include in his analysis only as much of a situation as happens to suit his purposes.

Consider the "situation" involved in dropping atomic bombs on Hiroshima and Nagasaki. The usual defense of this action—a utilitarian argument—is that it saved lives by hastening the end of Japanese resistance. If the situation is considered in this very narrow framework, the conclusion seems logical and the atomic-bombing of the two cities was a moral action. However, it is equally logical to take into consideration other consequences (the killing of civilians, the unloosing of a new and particularly horrible instrument of violence, and so forth) and reach the opposite conclusion that this action was immoral. In situationism he who defines the situation also and automatically determines the moral verdict.

. Again, in telling an individual to act in a way that will

bring about the most good for the largest number of people, the new morality does not offer much help as to which people it has in view. Does this apply only to people who have been born? It makes a difference—for example, in determining the morality of abortion (where most of the new morality advocates would exclude the unborn from consideration) or in judging the morality of fallout-producing nuclear tests (where many new morality people, adverting to the danger of genetic damage, would reverse field and include unborn future generations in their moral calculation). Consistency is not a notable trait of this school of ethical thought.

Yet the fact remains that the new morality has a powerful appeal today, particularly when it employs the eye-catching slogan that "love alone is the standard of morality." Who can be against love? It is like being against pretty women and apple pie.

But those who argue that love is all do not sufficiently consider the tremendous ambiguities involved in the use of the word "love." Just which "love" is involved? In one sense everyone loves himself and others, and everyone always acts out of love. The difference between a moral and an immoral disposition is not whether one loves and acts on the basis of love, but how one loves. Presumably the public executioner loves the condemned man; it makes a considerable difference, however, whether—and why—he does or does not kill him.

In another sense love is a sentiment, a feeling. Happily it is a feeling which almost everyone experiences at some time or another in his life and perhaps at many times. But the experience of being in love has nothing to do with morality directly, even though it can well prove the point of departure for moral goodness.

When we look into our own hearts, we find not one love but many. Each makes a more or less plausible claim to getting its way by controlling our choices and our actions, but in fact our diverse loves often are more or less in conflict with one another. A man loves his country and he also loves his own life. Is he therefore acting morally or immorally in risking his well-loved life to defend his well-loved country?

The conflict of loves within us is simply the beginning of the moral problem. If we had only one, dominant love, we would never have to ask ourselves the question "What is my true responsibility?" It is because conflicting loves make conflicting claims upon us that we must wrestle with moral problems. We are forced to seek a standard for making moral judgments, and this seeking is the beginning of ethics. To say "Follow love" is not an ethics at all but a refusal to take ethical problems seriously.

There is nevertheless a kernel of truth in the love-ethic which lends it attractiveness. If we were perfectly good—if, that is, we loved in a fully open and generous way all of the goods that together make up the human person, and if our whole personality were integrated into harmony with this attitude, and if, further, we lived among other people who were just like us in this—then (and only then) we would not need any criterion of morality beyond ourselves.

"Follow love" would make perfect sense, because our love would be a perfectly reliable moral guide. Confronted with alternatives, we would always make the morally right choice because nothing wrong (disordered, unbalanced, exaggerated) would have made any inroads in us. We would in fact "sense" what was right, much as a healthy person "senses" without reflection the appropriate movements and responses necessary to keep his balance. This, in sum, is the meaning of St. Augustine's often quoted (and almost as often misunderstood) words, "Love God and then do what you will."

Unfortunately, none of us seems to have arrived yet at the state of perfection just described. Some men are closer, some further from it; none is there yet. For those of us whose love is more or less imperfect, the advice to follow love really amounts to saying, "Do what you please." Many rationalizations, some of them sprinkled with fine rhetoric and, in particular, with frequent use of the word "love," can be found for doing what one pleases. But in the end, to do what one pleases is to do what one pleases; it is not an ethical position. Rather, it is ethical nonsense and moral chaos.

If we are to act morally, we need moral guidelines. Reason is admittedly a weak instrument in this area, but when all is said and done it is the only one we have. Without falling into the trap of supposing that our love *is* perfect, we must ask ourselves what we would do if our love *were* perfect. This is the ethical question, the answers to which will make it possible to develop sound ethical rules for living our lives. And next we shall examine the question—and its answers—in some detail.

Questions for review and discussion

1. John Dewey says situations present problems—felt evils to be dealt with. What is presupposed by the perception of a set of facts as evil?

2. Utilitarianism is based on the application of a technical model to human action—it amounts to thinking of all human action as if it were second-level action. How does this sort of theory have a legitimate application?

3. Why do you suppose a theory such as utilitarianism became so popular in the past and present century?

4. Using situation ethics, think of opposite decisions that might be made on the morality of important current issues. Show how either decision, once made, can be given a plausible utilitarian justification.

5. Is it possible for the same person consistently to hold to subjectivism and utilitarianism in his ethics?

6. Distinguish and exemplify as many different senses of "love" as you can.

7. Explain what is involved in the ideal case of perfect love. Do you think anyone ever approaches or has ever approached this ideal? Are there instances in your own experience in which your love of the good was sufficient to make you see the right thing to do—and do it—without even asking yourself what was the "right" thing?

8. Authors who advocate situation ethics often use examples involving sexual morality. Can you think of any reason why they should concentrate on examples from this field?

9. Some advocates of situation ethics claim it is Christian morality, and that for Christians the only moral absolute is the demand to do what love requires. How does this square with your reading of the New Testament?

11: Guidelines for Love

Moral rules have a bad reputation today. The preceding chapter suggests why this is so. A state of affairs in which moral rules are necessary is less than ideal, and many people today wish to make a dramatic leap into the ideal. Sad to say, however, human beings do not seem to be ideal, which is why moral rules are necessary. People who have 20/20 vision do not need to wear eyeglasses, but those with imperfect vision find them a necessity. Morally speaking, all of us have imperfect vision. Moral rules help us to compensate for our imperfection and see more clearly.

To see more clearly in this case is to know with some degree of exactness what our concrete moral responsibilities are. In what follows we do not try to provide a moral handbook, a neat summary of common moral responsibilities. The concrete responsibilities of each individual are different, and these are what is important. We cannot tell each individual what *his* responsibilities are, and we would not wish to take on such a task even if it were possible.

What we do try to provide is assistance for the individual who wishes to think through his own life and come to understand his responsibilities better. As we have seen, the basic principle of morality is, One ought always to choose inclusivistically. The question is, How does this basic principle take shape in the differing bodies of moral responsibilities of each person?

Modes of responsibility

The moral guidelines we will discuss here do not make up a handbook of common responsibilities, as we have said. These guidelines might instead be described as general principles from which each person can develop his own detailed moral code; they are also principles by which any existing or possible moral code can be criticized. Since these principles shape and control moral responsibilities, we call them "modes of responsibility." We will deal with six such modes in this chapter; two others of extreme importance and complexity will receive separate treatment in the chapters that follow.

If one's attitude toward all the fundamental human purposes were open and inclusivistic (the basic criterion of moral goodness), he would not live for passing satisfactions or for specific future objectives. He would instead commit himself to the realization of basic purposes with which he could identify to such an extent that the free actions by which he realized them would in fact constitute him as the person he was. Furthermore, he would make a number of such commitments—large, third-level actions like marrying or engaging in a profession. And, further still, he would strive to make his commitments consistent with one another, so that they formed a harmonious framework for his life. This, then, is the first mode of responsibility: consistent commitment to a harmonious set of purposes or values.

Negatively, this mode of responsibility rules out a certain kind of premoral spontaneity, in which a man in effect puts himself at the service of a desire or inclination which is not harmonized with the rest of his fundamental life-purposes. Many people do in fact spend a great part of their lives in the service of such goals—pleasure, wealth, status, and so forth—which do not represent rational commitments but instead originated as mere wants or cravings. Such unreflective, slavish activity has nothing to do with a free, self-determined life.

At the same time there is a place for spontaneity within morality. For the individual who has integrated his commitments into a consistent pattern, spontaneous action within this pattern becomes almost second nature. But spontaneity in this case will be in line with one's commitments rather than something that precedes commitment. From the perspective of this mode of responsibility, immorality consists in using one's mature powers in the service of infantile goals, while morality means organizing one's life around basic commitments and acting within the pattern one has created by this organization.

A second mode of responsibility is that if one has an open and inclusivistic attitude toward all the fundamental human purposes, he will at all times take into account all of the goods, and will, furthermore, do so not merely as they apply to himself but as they apply to all other men. He will not regard himself as a special case, demanding concessions and special treatment he is unwilling to grant to others. He will regularly ask himself questions such as "How would I like it if somebody did this to me?" and "What would happen if everybody acted as I wish to act?"

It is no secret that this moral rule is violated frequently in ordinary experience. Violations are especially common on the part of people who have undergone a change in their state of life and no longer remember how things looked "on the other side." How many parents, one wonders, inflict injustices on their children which they, as children suffering the same injustices at the hands of *their* parents, vowed never to be guilty of in adult life?

A third mode of responsibility, also involving relationships with others, might be described simply as openness: willingness to help others, desire to see them develop and perfect themselves by realizing to the fullest the goods of which they are capable. A person with this attitude is not defensive or selfish about protecting his own position of excellence or superiority in relation to others.

A striking example is provided by the good teacher who genuinely rejoices in seeing his students progress in their particular discipline or skill, even if the students come in time to outshine the teacher. A man with this attitude will also accept and take satisfaction in the ways in which other people are different from him; he will not demand that everyone mirror his tastes and enthusiasms.

Morality, from the viewpoint of this mode of responsibility, is often expressed in willingness to accept responsibility for the needs of another even where there is no structured relationship with the other which compels one to do so. Conversely, immorality is apparent in the actions of persons who feel no responsibility for others with whom they come into contact in unstructured relationships (e.g., the driver who does not stop or send help back to a stranded motorist). To insist on having a clear-cut duty before doing what is necessary to help someone else reflects an immoral attitude.

Detachment and fidelity

"Detachment" is the word which characterizes a fourth mode of responsibility. Its contrary is manifested by people who are so oriented toward one purpose that its frustration or loss is a shattering experience which drains their lives of meaning. Someone with a morally good attitude, an openness to all human goods, will not be so totally destroyed by the loss of any one good, no matter how genuinely painful the loss may be. Put in terms of levels of action, what the fourth mode of responsibility says is that one should never regard the specific and limited objective of a second-level action as if it were the human good itself to which one is committed and in which one participates through a third-level action.

A person with a religious turn of mind may object at this point that what has just been said cannot apply to loving God above all else—something to which every man ought to be totally dedicated, and dedicated above everything else. This is true, so long as one keeps in mind that God is not an aspect of the human personality, that God transcends all human goods, and that, properly understood, love of God implies love of all human goods; implies, in other words, precisely the morally good attitude we have been attempting to describe. However, it *is* possible to overidentify with and overcommit oneself to the human good of religion, in which case the aberration in question is what is called "religious fanaticism."

The fifth mode of responsibility complements detachment. While prepared to accept the loss of particular satisfactions and achievements without regarding this as a final loss of his personhood, a man should nevertheless remain committed to his ideals. He should, in other words, practice fidelity. A person with such an attitude will persist in seeking to realize realistically realizable purposes; by contrast, a person with an immoral attitude will tend to give up rather easily upon encountering problems and obstacles.

Fidelity or stability in commitment to purposes is not the same thing as mere constancy, much less rigidity. It implies continuing effort to explore new ways of better serving the purposes to which one is committed. Further-more, it involves refusal to narrow down a human good to those particular expressions of it with which one happens to be familiar. A creative and open approach to living is not only consistent with but essential to genuine fidelity.

Put in terms of levels of action, what this fifth mode of responsibility—fidelity—means is that one should never re-gard the human goods themselves to which one is com-mitted and in which one participates through his free self-determination in third-level actions as if those goods were merely the specific, limited, extrinsic objectives of second-level actions.

Detachment on the one hand and fidelity on the other balance each other in the life of an individual. They enable a man to strike a mean between the immoral extremes of fanaticism and noninvolvement. They also rule out an attitude of unwillingness to attempt difficult things and thereby risk failure.

Morality does not require one to take needless risks or to be unrealistic about circumstances, including one's own abilities, and the consequent chances of failing in an under-taking. But a person with a morally good attitude will be inclined to push beyond what he and others have already accomplished and to take reasonable chances in the pro-cess, aware that many good and important things in life will never be done except by people who are willing to run the risk of failing in the attempt to do them.

Pursuit of limited objectives

Under the sixth mode of responsibility one will seek specific ends which contribute to realization of the broader, deeper purposes to which he has dedicated his life. The pursuit of specific objectives which can be attained by definite, limited means should always be included within the framework of our basic self-constitution.

This may seem a surprising thing to say in view of the many occasions on which we have up to now criticized the pursuit of limited objectives. The point of this criticism, however, has been that it is wrong to limit one's morality, and one's life, merely to this. But, provided life is grounded upon and built around commitment to a consistent set of purposes, it is not only good sense but one's responsibility to, as it were, put flesh on the bones of these commitments by pursuing limited ends which further their realization.

Thus a man with a morally good attitude will indeed be efficient and will in a sense live by the utilitarian code (although not *alone* by the utilitarian code): where there is no other moral issue, act to achieve the most good or to avoid the most harm.

The genuine utilitarian, of course, assumes that there never is any other moral issue—that is, that the moral value of alternative acts can always be established by comparing their consequences and weighing the benefits and harms on a merely quantitative scale. As we have seen, this approach to morality as such will not work. But where comparisons are possible, as sometimes happens (when one is confronted with different ways of realizing the same good), it is both appropriate and morally responsible to make them.

Where, morally speaking, efficiency is possible, it is a virtue, although it is no virtue if it means achieving a limited objective at the expense of violating some basic good. Waste and inefficiency, by contrast, are signs of vice, although it is no vice to be judged "inefficient" in the pursuit of an objective when "efficiency" would require the violation of fundamental human goods.

Thus a nation might be judged inefficient in defending itself against aggression, even to the point of allowing itself to be overrun and conquered. But there would be nothing immoral about such inefficiency—it would in fact reflect an entirely moral attitude—if the efficiency in question came down in cold fact to repelling the aggression by merciless bombing of the potential invader's civilian population.

The modes of responsibility, as the last example suggested, apply not only to individuals but also to communities in their common action. In other words, they hold not only for men singly but for men collectively. Each mode of responsibility has a social as well as an individual dimension.

It is worth noting, too, that various ethical or pseudo-ethical theories have seized upon one (or some) of these modes of responsibility in isolation from the rest and have attempted to make it (or them) the sole criterion of morality. This is the case, for instance, with utilitarianism, which attempts to reduce all of morality to the sixth mode of responsibility (efficiency).

Many moral theories similarly go wrong, not so much by basing themselves on false principles as by taking too limited a view of moral principles and excluding others equally as valid. By ignoring other principles—other modes of responsibility—they fall into the trap of exclusivity, which is ultimately fatal to moral goodness. (This is not to say, of course, that the men who proposed these theories were morally evil men; it is only to say that the theories will not lead people to moral goodness as the men who proposed them intended that they should.)

Goodness will not be found in respecting one mode of responsibility only, any more than it will be found in respecting only one basic human good. Instead, moral goodness demands recognition and observance of all the modes of responsibility we have discussed here—and two we shall examine in the chapters that follow—at the same time.

Questions for review and discussion

1. Would you rate the first mode of responsibility—consistent commitment to a harmonious set of purposes—relatively easy or one of the more difficult ones to fulfill? Why?

2. Kant, who bases his ethics on the second mode of responsibility, rejects as too narrow the formulation "Do unto others as you would have them do unto you." Instead he offers the formulation "Act so that the maxim of your action can at the same time serve as a universal law." Compare these formulations with each other and with the formulation offered in the text.

3. Can you think of striking examples in which the third mode of responsibility (willingness to help others and accept responsibility for their needs) is fulfilled? In which it is violated?

4. Detachment and fidelity (the fourth and fifth modes of responsibility) seem to go in opposite directions. The idea is to exclude fanaticism on the one hand and noninvolvement on the other. Discuss concrete cases which illustrate the difficulty—yet also the possibility—of steering a middle course between these two extremes.

5. Do you think it likely that a detached person will sometimes seem cold and unenthusiastic and that a faithful person will sometimes seem overzealous and almost fanatic? What are the signs of real detachment and fidelity?

6. The sixth mode of responsibility—to act efficiently to realize specific objectives—corresponds to the utilitarian outlook. As a mode of responsibility, in our sense, how does it differ from being the very principle of morality itself?

7. In this chapter we illustrate the sixth mode of responsibility with an example that applies to a society rather than to an individual. Illustrate the other five modes with examples which also apply to societies of various kinds.

8. Can you think of reasons for the tendency to build an entire ethics around one or two modes of responsibility and neglect the others?

9. Moral arguments typically move from a discussion of what is involved in a particular action, and the facts of the case, back to some assumed moral rules, which are then criticized by appealing to modes of responsibility. Analyze some examples of actual or fictional moral arguments which reveal this pattern.

12: Duties: Responsibilities
in Community

In many people's minds "duty" and "morality" are virtually synonymous, and doing your duty is the sum and substance of moral goodness. As we have seen, there is a great deal more to morality than this. But the fact remains that duty is an extremely important mode of responsibility, and one which is also extremely complex.

Duties are essentially social. They arise in structured relationships with other people. (In passing, it should be said that the concept of "duty" applies not only to individuals but to communities as well; a community can have duties with regard to individual persons and also with regard to other communities.) Basically, there are two kinds of duty.

One might be called "contractual duty." As the name suggests, it arises on the basis of a contract or agreement. A man wants to achieve a certain objective and needs someone else's help. In order to get the help, he agrees to do something for the other person in return. (For example, a man wants his house painted and agrees to pay the painter to do the job.) In such a situation each party to the agreement has a duty to fulfill his part of the bargain.

There will be exceptions, of course. For example, one has no responsibility for carrying out an agreement to do something that is morally wrong. A hired gunman has no real duty to kill the person he is paid to assassinate. Again, responsibility under a contract disappears when circumstances change in such a way that it would be disastrous for one of the parties to fulfill the agreement. A circus tightrope walker is not required to go up on the high wire when he feels dizzy, even in order to meet the terms of his contract with the circus management.

However, no special mode of responsibility beyond those we have already considered seems necessary to deal with contractual duties. In order to see why one should generally keep one's agreements it is enough to consider that this is the way one would want others to treat oneself (the second mode of responsibility considered in the previous chapter). Unless there is general assent that "Do unto others as you would have them do unto you" is a valid moral principle, there can be no workable contracts and agreements; for otherwise it would be necessary to assume that agreements are only made to be broken.

Generally speaking, contracts and agreements similar to them represent the coordination of peoples' actions at the second level of action. The actions required under contracts are specific means to specific objectives. Contracts are immensely important, indeed essential, in everyday life; but, morally speaking, they do not raise many special problems and they are not very interesting. Far more difficult and significant, in ethical terms, is the question of duty as it relates to social relationships involving and based upon third-level action.

Communities and duties

Each of us has a variety of social roles arising from membership in various communities, and each of these social roles carries with it a variety of duties. To see why these duties normally are real *moral* responsibilities (why, that is, they concern good and evil and why they involve our self-determination) it is necessary to bear in mind what constitutes a genuine community.

A crowd of people brought together by accident or force—by something extrinsic to the members of the group—is not a community. A community is constituted instead by a kind of third-level act in which two or more people engage together so that it becomes in a real way their action in common. A community is characterized by shared commitment on the part of its members to the realization of some fundamental human purpose or purposes and by structures and activity appropriate to bringing this about.

In many respects a family is a model community. Its members are joined by ties of blood and mutual dependence, to be sure, but also by a joint commitment to common purposes of a very basic and intimate sort. Where such a commitment is lacking, a particular family may exist as a socioeconomic unit—as a kind of convenient arrangement—but it is not a genuine "community" as the word is understood and used here.

Definite structures and activity are required for the realization of the purposes which constitute a community. Institutions are necessary to articulate the purposes to which the community members are committed. All this in turn gives rise to various roles—what one might call "job descriptions"—for the different community members. Within the family, for instance, "father" refers to one role, "mother" to another, "eldest son" to a third, and so on.

The fulfillment of these roles will require that the persons filling them act in certain ways. These required ways of acting are duties, and a duty may be defined as something one has a responsibility for doing or not doing by virtue of one's role in a particular community. Just as we all have many social roles, so we have many duties: as a student, as a citizen, as a family member, as an employer or employee, and so on.

A community cannot function efficiently if its members do not live up to their roles and fulfill their duties. But true as this is, it is not this which makes duties genuine moral responsibilities. The aspect of moral responsibility enters in, rather, because of the fact that the members of a community are engaged in a joint third-level action seeking the realization of a fundamental human purpose or purposes.

A community member who does not fulfill his role and live up to his duties is in effect seeking to enjoy participation in the common good for which the community is organized without putting into it what is required of him if the community is to continue to realize the good for which it exists. He is trying to get something for nothing, to enjoy a free ride, at the expense of the other community members. Moreover, he is undermining the community at its roots by refusing to do his part to realize its purposes. If enough members behave in this way, the result, sooner or later, will be the collapse of the community and the end of the possibility that *this* community will realize its constituting purposes.

When one reflects on the attitude of the community member who refuses or neglects to carry out his duties, it becomes apparent that in reality he cares less about the good upon which the community is grounded than about his own enjoyment of that good. He is in the community for what he can get out of it, not for what he can contribute to joint realization of the community's shared commitment. His attitude toward other members of the community is basically exploitative: he seeks to use them in order to realize his self-interest instead of working with them and for them in order that all together may participate more fully in the purpose which brought them together. Such an exploitative attitude is fundamentally inimical to and destructive of community.

This point also can be explained in terms of the levels of action. A community is constituted by a shared commitment, which is at the third level of action. A member who does not do his duty transforms his own action from third-level participation in the common good to an action at the second level, directed now to the limited objective of getting what he can get for himself out of the situation. Such a person naturally hopes that other members of the community will continue to fulfill their duties in a dedicated way.

Having said this, however, it is necessary to add two important qualifications. First, our duties as community members are real moral responsibilities only if the community itself is a genuine one. Second, when duties conflict with one another—as they sometimes do—our moral responsibility is limited to fulfilling only one of the conflicting duties, but deciding which one is not at all easy. Both of these points deserve a closer look.

In search of community

A pure community in which there are no elements of injustice and exploitation is a very rare thing. Indeed, it is doubtful whether such a phenomenon ever does exist in our imperfect world. Certainly, the large-scale societies of which we are all members are not pure communities. They have aspects of genuine community, but they have less attractive aspects as well. And our duties as members of such a society are true moral responsibilities only when they arise from the community aspect of the society rather than from its unjust and exploitative aspects.

Nations, including the United States, are such societies, partly community and partly a highly complex structure to facilitate self-interest and exploitation. To say this is not to engage in breast-beating or viewing with alarm; it is simply to state the evident fact of the matter.

As a community, the United States is some two hundred million people joined in a commitment to realize a number of noble purposes which find verbal expression in such formulations as the Preamble to the Constitution. But while this joint commitment is certainly an aspect of the reality of the nation, it is not the total picture. Side by side with it one finds ample evidence that some individuals and groups receive preferred treatment.

Loopholes in the tax laws, for example, allow some segments of society to escape most taxes while other citizens find their taxes soaring; the simple fact of being born with white skin instead of black or brown or yellow tends to ensure one of certain privileges and prerogatives which black-, brown-, and yellow-skinned people enjoy only rarely and with great difficulty, if at all.

Quite simply, one can take it for granted that any large society will be only an approximation of a true community. At its best it will be an expression of community. At its worst it will be a system for exploitation. Between its best and its worst it will be a system of more or less fair deals and arrangements into which community degenerates under the erosive power of exploitation.

What does all this imply as far as our duties as members of such societies are concerned? Simply that such duties are real moral responsibilities only to the extent that they flow from our roles in institutions which articulate the fundamental commitment of the society-as-community. On the other hand, to the extent that duties arise from some form of institutionalized exploitation they are not moral responsibilities, and in some cases one may even have the responsibility of refusing to carry out such a duty.

An example makes this clearer. Slavery is an extreme form of institutionalized exploitation, yet slavery has been accepted in many societies throughout history. Even the United States, which articulated its belief in and commitment to essential human equality at the time of its founding, simultaneously recognized the institution of slavery and sanctioned it in law.

A slave, as a member of such a society, has a duty to submit to his enslavement; and this duty will be embodied in laws which provide, among other things, for his punishment if he is a bad slave. Yet no one seriously supposes today that this duty carries with it any real moral responsibility. In short, in a society which accepts slavery as a social institution some people may have a social duty to be slaves but they can have no moral responsibility arising from this role, and it is not immoral of them to refuse their duty.

The example of slavery is a case in which societies have given institutional expression—of a rather extreme variety—to exploitation, and the consequent social duties are not moral responsibilities. But there are other cases as well in which social duty does not carry any moral responsibility. For example, it sometimes happens that the purposes of a society which one joined voluntarily change. In such a case one has a moral responsibility only in regard to duties which reflect the purposes of the society at the time one accepted membership in it; one has no responsibility to fulfill duties which reflect new purposes to which one does not subscribe.

If, for example, one joins a recreational club, and the club later begins to change its orientation to some form of political activism, the mere fact that one is a member of the club does not impose any moral responsibility to join in its political activities if one has not subscribed to this new orientation.

Something similar occurs when changing circumstances bring about a change in the division of labor within the society. Over a period of time, perhaps, the amount of effort required in one area diminishes while that involved in another area increases greatly, so that after a while some members of the group find themselves doing very little work and others doing a great deal. In such a case something like exploitation has crept into the society without anyone's really intending it. When this happens it is time for the society to take a fresh look at the situation and redivide the duties. And if the beneficiaries of the imbalance refuse to do so (as sometimes happens), the victims have no moral responsibility to continue to carry out their duties.

Even this abbreviated discussion should make it apparent that this is a very complicated subject. While it is easy enough to say in the abstract that duties that arise from exploitative social institutions are not moral responsibilities, in reality it may be irresponsible not to tolerate a certain amount of injustice in society. The tax laws, for instance, may not be totally just, but if everyone stopped paying his taxes for this reason—or felt free to cheat on his tax return—the result would more likely be chaos than reform. Achieving and constantly maintaining perfect balance and perfect justice in the ever-changing conditions of a society are simply not possible.

Knowing when to comply with duties that lack the force of moral responsibilities and when to refuse to comply often requires a subtle discernment which cannot be programmed in advance. But it should be clear at least that not every social duty is also a moral responsibility and that one may at times have a right to refuse to carry out some duties. In fact, if carrying out a particular duty would be immoral on other grounds, one's moral responsibility is to refuse to carry it out. This is the principle of conscientious objection.

When duties conflict

Equally complicated is the situation of an individual whose duties as a member of different communities come into conflict with each other. A businessman is scheduled to make an important out-of-town trip for his company; the day before he is to leave, his wife comes down with a bad case of the flu. If he does not make the trip, a deal on which his company has been counting is likely to fall through; if he does make the trip, his wife will have to go on taking care of the house and children when she ought properly to be in bed. What should he do—go or stay?

There is no a priori answer to that question. Taken individually, each duty here would be a moral responsibility. But the duties now are in head-on conflict. The answer will be different for different individuals, but there are certain guidelines which are applicable to any such case.

For one thing, if it is not really impossible to fulfill both duties, one has a moral responsibility to do so, but if it is really impossible, one does not have a moral responsibility to do so. One is never morally responsible for doing the impossible. Furthermore, since either of the conflicting duties would be a moral responsibility if it were not for the other, one has a definite moral responsibility to fulfill one or the other of the duties. The businessman-husband of our example is morally responsible either to make the trip or to stay home with his wife; he may not cop out by refusing to do either. Further still, there are no general principles by which one can say that the weight of moral responsibility lies in the direction of one duty or the other. Since both are serious duties, the individual will be doing the morally right thing if he does either one.

However, he should be honest in making his choice. For one thing, this means that if an individual in such a conflict situation considers how he would feel if he were in the position of each of the others involved, and opts in a way he would really consider unreasonable if he were in one of the other positions, then he may be violating another mode of responsibility, the second one.

Moreover, it is reasonable to doubt an individual's honesty if on many occasions he always opts for one set of duties and against the other. In the example given it may be that the businessman consistently puts his job before his family. If that is the case, and if in this situation, too, he chooses the job-related duty in preference to the family-related one, it is likely that his choice is really an expression of a selfish bias rather than an honest judgment of moral responsibility.

In addition, persons faced with conflicting duties should take practical steps to try to resolve their quandary. Perhaps, if he tried, the businessman could postpone his trip after all; or perhaps he can make arrangements for his wife's sister to come and care for her and the children while he is out of town.

People in such situations should also try to discuss their problem with the other parties involved in order to get their suggestions and also to determine so far as possible who will be most hurt by the nonfulfillment of duty. Perhaps the businessman will discover that his colleagues do not consider the trip to be as important as he does or that his wife is really not so terribly sick and does not object to his leaving.

Fundamentally, the fact that duties can and sometimes do conflict suggests that an individual should exercise great care in making commitments and in accepting membership in different communities. It is rash to take on a variety of social roles carrying duties which one might with forethought have known would come into conflict. In practice, this means that a person should attempt to organize his life so that, as far as possible, his various roles and duties will complement and support each other instead of conflicting.

It reflects not only good planning but a morally correct attitude when a man's family life, career, civic and church responsibilities, and other social roles mesh in a harmonious and consistent way. To be sure, no one can be so farseeing as to eliminate conflicts of duty from his life entirely, and in our society it is more difficult for some people—for example, more difficult for some women than for men. But it is not only sensible but a moral responsibility to try to prevent conflicts as much as possible and, when inevitable conflicts do arise, to act with a combination of honesty and practicality in attempting to resolve them.

Up to now we have considered seven of the modes of responsibility. The eighth is yet to come. It is the subject of the next chapter.

Questions for review and discussion

1. If moral responsibility is limited to duty, what sort of theory is likely to result?

2. If duties were the only mode of responsibility, would cultural relativism (or relativity of morals to each society) be true?

3. Contractual duties are fairly obvious forms of responsibility, and sometimes an effort has been made to ground all duties in a

"social contract." What do such attempts imply concerning the theory of the individual and society?

4. It has been suggested that even the duties which arise from genuine community can be reduced to other modes of responsibility, such as the second and the fifth, so that no separate, seventh mode of responsibility is needed. Discuss this point of view.

5. Our section entitled "In search of community" suggests, but does not spell out, a theory of social justice. Can you articulate this theory more clearly? Compare it with classic theories such as the following: (1) that each individual should receive from the society according to his merit (Aristotle); (2) that each should contribute according to his ability and receive according to his needs (Marx); and (3) that each should promote as far as possible the equality of all members (liberal democracy).

6. Some ethical theories suppose that there can be a conflict of moral responsibilities. How does our position on conflict of duties differ?

7. In case of conflict of duties how might it help to invoke other modes of responsibility, such as the second one?

8. Think of actual or fictional examples of conflict of duties and discuss the manner in which they were resolved.

9. Sartre suggests as typical of the situation of moral choice a case in which a young man during World War II must decide either to stay with his aged mother who needs his care or join his friends in the French underground. He points out that the young man's commitment alone will determine which is right, and from this concludes that moral responsibility is subjective. Criticize this line of argument in light of what we have learned about duties.

13: Persons, Means, and Ends

Are there ethical absolutes? Are there principles which should never be violated and therefore things which should never be done, regardless of circumstances and consequences?

Most people, almost instinctively, would answer Yes, and would then go on to cite some action which they feel should never be performed: purposely to torture a small child, for instance. Yet for many ethical theorists in our times the answer is No. For them there are no ethical absolutes and therefore no actions which can flatly be ruled out as being beyond the pale of acceptable human behavior.

This is not to suggest that such theorists are themselves vicious or immoral. People who do not believe in ethical absolutes may indeed be high-minded and right-living—in particular cases more so perhaps than individuals who hold that there are some actions which ought never to be performed.

But the issue is not whose private life and personal

behavior are more upstanding and blameless. The question is, rather, Whose ethical position is true? Is any action whatsoever allowable, at least in certain circumstances? Or are there actions which it is never morally right to perform?

Our eighth mode of responsibility states unequivocally that there are such actions. It may be put quite simply: it is never right to act directly against one of the fundamental human goods. But while it is easy enough to state this principle, it is more difficult to show what it means. The question is far removed from idle speculation, however. Indeed, it is one of the most burning ethical issues of our times, an issue of far-reaching practical ramifications for individual and social life.

Duties and responsibilities

In our discussion of duties we saw that many of our moral responsibilities arise from duties (which in turn arise from our structured social relationships with other people). Such responsibilities have true moral force, but they are not absolute. This is evident in the fact that they can and sometimes do conflict with one another. A man's responsibilities arising from his duties as a husband may sometimes come into conflict with his responsibilities as an employee. Both sets of duties are real, but in a particular situation an individual may not be able to respond to both.

In such a case a person must fulfill one set of duties and neglect the other. Provided he is being honest about the facts and his response to the facts, he can do so with a clear conscience, in the knowledge that these duties, while real, are not absolute responsibilities and, where circumstances require, can be neglected in favor of other, equally pressing duties.

However, there are other responsibilities which do not arise from duties and which are not conditional but absolute. They are founded instead on the implications of the ideal of openness to all the goods constitutive of the human person. Openness to the human goods is the basis of a right moral attitude.

In acting directly against any one of them we make that against which we act a means to an ulterior end. But the goods that go to make up personhood are themselves the ends of human action, and as such they should not be treated as if they were mere means to other ends. Because each of these goods is, as we have seen, the supreme good in its own way, no one of them can be subordinated to another as a means to an end. Thus the minimum requirement for a morally correct attitude (and action) is simultaneous respect for all the basic goods: respect which means in practice refusing to violate any fundamental good in order to achieve another.

The seven modes of responsibility we have examined previously are positive: they tell us what to do. But this eighth mode is negative. It tells us what we ought *not* to do. It is not correct to suppose that all morality is summed up in prohibitions ("thou shalt not"), even though it is sometimes caricatured that way. But it is also a mistake to overlook the extremely strong binding force of this negative mode of responsibility: one should never act directly against any of the fundamental human goods.

It is essential to remember that these goods are what human life and human action are all about. The goods are not abstractions existing "out there" beyond us and other people. Rather, as we experience them, the goods are aspects of human persons, ourselves or others, aspects which either already exist in actuality or have the potential of being realized. Thus, to act directly against one of the fundamental goods is to violate an actual or possible aspect of the personhood of a real person or persons: to violate "life," for example, means violating somebody's life. This amounts to using a human person as a means to an end.

Are there inalienable rights?

Critics of the view that there are ethical absolutes sometimes refer to them disparagingly as "legalistic absolutes." Rhetoric aside, the implication is that this position exalts law (legalism) at the expense of the person. Yet the defense of ethical absolutes, properly understood, does not mean assigning primacy to bloodless law over flesh-and-blood persons. On the contrary, it constitutes a defense of the person and his inalienable rights.

If there are no absolute responsibilities, there are no inalienable rights. If it were true that any action, no matter what, is permitted in certain circumstances, then no good intrinsic to the person would be safe from invasion and suppression provided the justifying circumstances existed. In such a case it would always be possible to conceive of circumstances in which the person could be sacrificed to the attainment of ulterior ends.

Instead of being the norm and source from which other things receive their value, the human person would become simply one more item or commodity with a relative value, inviolable only up to the point at which it became expedient to violate him in order to achieve some objective. It would then make no sense at all to speak of the "infinite value" of the human person. Far from being infinite, the value of a person would be quite specific and quantifiable, something to be weighed calculatingly in the balance against other values.

Often it is assumed that this sort of weighing of human goods (and human persons) is possible. This assumption enters in, tacitly in many instances, as a result of confusion between the fundamental goods constitutive of the person, which are always open-ended and never fully defined (because one can never say that one of these goods has been totally realized and exhausted by oneself or others), and a specific objective which is never completely identical with the person.

Typically, an individual with such an attitude will think along the following lines: Two lives are better than one; therefore if two innocent lives can be saved by sacrificing one innocent life, it is entirely right and proper to sacrifice the one life in order to save the two.

An example dramatizes this attitude. In wartime a military commander is confronted with a group of prisoners who possess important information about the enemy's plans. He needs the information in order to prevent loss of life among his own men, but the prisoners will not tell him what he wants to know. In order to compel the prisoners to talk, he has one of them executed as an example to the others and thereby frightens the survivors into divulging the desired information. Thus, by taking one life he has saved other lives, and according to the principle that two lives are better than one (or twenty better than two, or two thousand better than twenty, and so on) his action is not only expedient but morally right.

One arrives at a very different judgment, however, if human life is regarded not as a concrete, specific, essentially quantifiable object but as a good in which each person participates but which none exhausts or sums up in himself. In such a view of reality it is simply not possible to make the sort of calculation which weighs lives against each other (my life is more valuable than John's life, John's life is more valuable than Ed's and Tom's combined, etc.) and thus determines whose life shall be respected and whose sacrificed. The value of life, each human life, is incalculable, not in any merely poetic sense but simply because it is something not susceptible to calculation, measurement, weighing, and balancing.

Traditionally this point has been expressed by the statement that the end does not justify the means. This is simply a way of saying that the direct violation of any good intrinsic to the person cannot be justified by the good result which such a violation will bring about. What is extrinsic to human persons may be used for the good of persons, but what is intrinsic to persons has a kind of sacredness and may not be violated.

Returning to our earlier analysis of human action, it should be apparent that the attitude which regards goods intrinsic to the person as inviolable corresponds to the third level of action: action, that is, directed to a fundamental human good as something in which one participates. On the other hand, the attitude that any good, any value, can be directly violated if circumstances require this in order to achieve another good corresponds to the second level of action: action in which the good is equated with specific objectives which one seeks to achieve by calculation.

Again, the first of these attitudes represents an inclusivistic approach in which one remains always open to all the goods, even though one cannot always act to realize each of them; while the second manifests an exclusivistic attitude in which the good not chosen becomes, by that fact, worthless. Using persons as mere means is always wrong because it betrays the fact that one does not love the whole constellation of human goods in an inclusivistic way, but rather loves this part as against that part: loves the part he chooses or furthers in preference to the part which he uses as his means.

Ethical absolutes and utilitarian solutions

Ultimately, of course, the conviction that there are no ethical absolutes and that, in consequence, there is no action which could not, in some circumstances, be morally justifiable represents a utilitarian approach to the question of ethics and action. In concluding this chapter it may be worth speculating on why this attitude has become so commonplace in our times and society and, in particular, why it is so evident in regard to the fundamental human good of life itself.

No one attempting an overview of the twentieth century can fail to be struck by the fact that something frightening has entered the picture in regard to attitudes toward human life (not the quality of life, but life itself). No doubt on some issues man's ethical sensitivity has moved forward in our times, but one can hardly make this judgment with regard to life. The massacre of millions of human beings in Hitler's Germany and Stalin's Russia is terrible evidence of the fact that at the very least the twentieth century has been no more respectful of life than past centuries, has, if anything, become more casual about the taking of life.

But what of our own society? The picture is no brighter here. It was the United States, after all, which dropped the first atomic bombs on Hiroshima and Nagasaki, justifying this action by the argument that it would "save lives" (American lives, of course, not Japanese lives, which presumably were judged to be of less value).

One might be tempted to dismiss the atomic bombing of these two cities as an isolated aberration, an action performed in the heat of wartime passion and regretted later. But it is not really possible to accept this explanation, for the fact of the matter is that for the past quarter-century the United States has put the world on notice that if circumstances so require, it is prepared to do to other cities and their civilian populations even worse than it did to Hiroshima and Nagasaki. That, after all, is what the U.S. nuclear deterrent strategy is all about: a strategy which affirms that, if pressed to the wall in war, the United States would rain down nuclear bombs on enemy cities. Leaving aside the question of whether such a course of action would in any sense be rational (although it would in fact be the height of irrationality), the strategy is built on the presumption that the United States really would do what it says it is prepared to do—otherwise the deterrent would not be credible.

Our intention here is not to enter into the intricacies of international politics and diplomacy. The point is simply that if the United States did what it says it is prepared to do (and the presumption must be that it is in deadly earnest about this), it would have performed an act of unparalleled immorality. In this case it is terrible to contemplate the judgment of future generations, if any.

We have, however, been living for years in the knowledge that this is the way in which the United States would, in certain circumstances, act. And it is submitted that, in subtle but real ways, this fact—of the nuclear deterrent strategy and all it implies—has undermined the foundations of moral perception and moral thought in our society. This is a broad statement and one whose truth is impossible to demonstrate in the confines of this parenthetical speculation. Yet it stands to reason that this appalling fact has, like a sort of moral disease, infected national life, deadened ethical sensitivity, and poisoned many aspects of our society.

We do not propose a solution here. We only suggest that the nuclear deterrent strategy represents a frighteningly logical application of the principle that the end *does* justify the means, and that, having accepted this principle as a fundamental premise in one crucial area of national life, we can hardly expect to be immune from its influence in many others as well.

Finally, it is necessary to acknowledge that acceptance of the principle that there are ethical absolutes—that the end does not justify the means—implies willingness to accept or tolerate some finite damage rather than act directly against one of the fundamental human goods. A nation unwilling to act unjustly in war, for example, may have to accept defeat.

Those who assert the position that the end does justify the means will frequently assert that this is unreasonable. But to one who is determined not to limit the meaning of human life to the quantifiable, who is determined instead to preserve the inviolability of the human person against threats and infringements, it will be the most reasonable thing in the world.

We have now considered all eight of the modes of responsibility. They do indeed give us moral guidelines; yet we are obliged to admit that applying them is not always a cut-and-dried matter. Doing so can in fact be excruciatingly hard in the case of action which is or seems to be ambiguous. In the next chapter we shall examine this difficult problem and see how it can be resolved.

Questions for review and discussion

1. What characteristic distinguishes the eighth mode of responsibility from the first seven?

2. Some who reject moral absolutes argue against them as legalism and say law is made for man, not man for the law. How can this challenge be answered within the framework of the present theory?

3. The eighth mode of responsibility leads to negative moral rules. Does the negative form of such rules point to a theoretical priority of evil over good?

4. There is a sense in which good ends do justify the means necessary to achieve them, provided these means are not in some way morally objectionable in themselves. With this in mind clarify the saying, "The end doesn't justify the means."

5. We mention in this chapter some military-political examples of the doctrine that the end does justify the means. Think of examples involving each of the categories of fundamental human purposes in which someone might be tempted to go directly against the good for the sake of some ulterior purpose.

6. One who holds the utilitarian point of view often will argue

against the eighth mode of responsibility by proposing examples in which there seems to be a huge disproportion between the damage done if one refuses to act directly against one of the goods which constitutes the person and the damage done if one does so act. Can you suggest a strategy to be used in dealing with such examples?

7. There was an ancient Stoic maxim "Let right be done, though the heavens fall." Is this a fair statement of the philosophy involved in the eighth mode of responsibility?

8. To what extent do you think it might be possible to accept the rest of the ethical theory outlined in this book and at the same time reject the eighth mode of responsibility? In other words, how much can be salvaged by someone who likes the approach in general but does not find himself able to agree with this last mode of responsibility?

14: When Action Is Ambiguous

Life is seldom as simple as one might wish. This is amply illustrated in ethics by problems that arise regarding an action which has more than one aspect. Looked at in one way, such an action seems to promote the realization of some human good and therefore appears itself ethically good. Looked at another way, it is destructive of a human good and therefore appears ethically evil.

How is one to evaluate an action with such built-in ambiguity? Is it proper to accentuate the positive and, concentrating on the good aspect, judge it to be morally good? Or is it ethically correct to place the emphasis on its evil aspect and judge it morally wrong? As a practical matter, may one or may one not perform such an action?

This is not a decision to be made casually or on the basis of a snap judgment. A person confronted with an apparent dilemma of this sort must take a close look at the action involved in order to determine what is really going on. Only on the basis of a clear-sighted analysis can one resolve the question of whether it is right or wrong to perform such an action.

Not either-or but both-and

It is important at this point to recall something said earlier. Morality is not a matter of external behavior alone, nor is it a matter of internal intention alone. Both are important, and in human action the two are inseparable. To determine the morality of an action a person must always answer two questions: "What am I doing? Why am I doing it?" It is not sufficient to ask and answer only one of these questions.

This point is important here because of the temptation some may feel to solve the problem of ambiguous action by saying that a good intention is by itself sufficient to make such an action morally good. This is the position taken, for example, by those who attempt to resolve what they often describe as the "agonizing dilemma" involved in the abortion decision by referring exclusively to the intention of the individual or individuals involved. Thus: "It is certainly repugnant to me that the unborn child should die, but that is not really my intention. I am only interested in sparing this woman avoidable pain and suffering."

It is not really that easy, however. As far as morality is concerned, the what and why of action are inseparable. Thus, in the case of abortion the *what* is the killing of an unborn human life; it is not possible for any *why*—that is, a good intention—to change this. (Furthermore, it should be noted in passing that reducing morality to a matter of intention alone opens the door dangerously wide to rationalizations of all sorts. A person can if he tries always find a good intention for what he is proposing to do, so that if good intentions were all that mattered it would be possible to justify doing almost anything.)

If, then, one cannot solve the problem of ambiguous action by relying simply on good intentions, it is necessary to find another approach. The key lies in closely examining the action involved to determine its real structure. If it is an indivisible unity and if it directly realizes a human good, then the person who performs the act for the sake of the good in which it allows him or someone else to participate need not be wrongly disposed toward the good which is simultaneously damaged; and provided he is not so disposed, his action might possibly be morally upright.

If, on the other hand, his intention does include damage to the good which is damaged, then he is acting wrongly in performing the act. If, furthermore, analysis of the action reveals that its two aspects are actually related to each other as means and end (the good result only is attained in an act distinct from that in which the bad is caused), then one must invoke the principle that the end does not justify the means and conclude that it is immoral to perform the action.

The previous sentences are packed with meaning and deal with complex matters. For the rest of this chapter we shall be attempting to explain what they say and why they say it.

Two kinds of ambiguity

As has just been suggested, the ambiguity of ambiguous action can be of two kinds. In one type the destructive aspect of the action is the means by which the positive aspect is realized. In the second the two aspects are really inseparably linked in one action; the positive aspect does not produce the destructive, nor does the destructive produce the positive; the one act embraces both results directly.

An example will help make this clearer. There was a time when boys with beautiful soprano voices were castrated so that their voices would not change and they could continue to sing in a choir. The action had two aspects: it was a mutilation of the human body, an attack upon an aspect of the basic good of life; it was also a *means* to facilitate the beautiful music which was intended to give glory to God. Clearly, however, the mutilation was one action and the production of the music a quite distinct action. Thus the two meanings of the initial action were not intrinsic to it; rather, an intrinsically mutilating act was only an extrinsic means to an end ultimately intended—namely, the beauty of the church service.

What was involved in this way of acting was that one fundamental human good (bodily integrity which is part of the good of life itself) was subordinated to others (aesthetic and religious). But it is immoral to subordinate basic goods to each other in such a way, since every one of these goods is an aspect of the human person and each of them is the supreme good in its own way. Thus, in the example given, the castration of the choir boys was not a morally justifiable thing to do. And this is so even though, presumably, the intention of those who did this was focused not on the destructive aspect of the action but on its positive effect.

Regardless of intention, the structure of action is what it is. It does not change simply because one's intention is directed toward one aspect rather than the other. Even though, in emotional terms, a person may not feel that he intends the destructive aspect of the action, nevertheless it is inescapable that he intend it inasmuch as it is required as the means to reaching the end toward which his feelings are directed.

Let us suppose, however, that a young boy is found to have a cancerous growth involving his testicles. To stop the disease requires that the boy be castrated. Here the act also has two aspects, but it is ambiguous in a different way from the previous example. On the one hand, the integrity of the body is damaged; part of the reality of a human life is literally cut off. But, on the other hand, in the very same act the life of the person is protected so far as possible from the destructive attack of the disease.

In this case one fundamental good—or aspect of a good—is not being sacrificed for another; the relationship between the two aspects is not that of means and end. Although the damage that is done by the operation is foreseen and fully understood, there is a very real sense in which it is inseparable from the good to which this very act makes its own immediate contribution. The operation is not castration done as a means to an ulterior good end, but cancer-removing surgery (which makes an immediate contribution to the good of life) that incidentally and unfortunately also is permanently mutilating. The operation is morally justifiable.

We wish to point out and to stress that a person can be so confused, in either his thinking or his feelings, that he is not fully aware of the real structure of his own action. Under pressure one can confuse the two sorts of ambiguous actions and thus imagine that he can act justifiably without adopting the maxim that the end justifies the means, while as a matter of fact only that maxim would rationalize what he does.

In particular cases such confusion can reduce or even entirely remove the personal guilt for the wrong acts that people do. However, a person who wants to act or at least to judge morally, and therefore rationally, will strive to overcome emotional and intellectual confusions so that he can analyze ambiguous actions carefully and make correct moral judgments in regard to them.

Killing the unborn

Many other examples can be taken to illustrate the difference between the two kinds of ambiguous action. For example, there is an important distinction to be made among operations done on pregnant women that result in death to the unborn. Some kill the unborn individual as a means to an ulterior end; others directly result in a benefit to the mother's health and only incidentally kill the unborn child.

If a woman does not want a baby because it would interfere with her career, or stretch the family budget too much, or cause her embarrassment, or for any other reason at all, and if she has an operation or does anything to get rid of the unwanted pregnancy, then this is killing as a means to an end. Such action goes directly against the fundamental good of human life itself and is morally wrong for that reason.

Since abortion is such a live issue, it is worth remarking in passing that it really doesn't matter whether one wishes to call the fetus a "person" or not. It is alive; it is human; it is an individual. No one can prove it is not a person, and it needs only to be let alone for a little while in order to prove to everyone that it is a person. The willingness to destroy the unborn is the willingness to destroy human life. No one would deny that this life is personal life except that there is pressure to kill it. Societies always find subtle grounds for questioning the personhood of those they wish to destroy. It happened before with the Blacks and the Indians; it is happening now with the unborn.

Yet there are cases in which it can be permissible to perform a procedure that results in the death of the unborn child, even when this outcome is known in advance. For instance, it may be necessary to remove a cancerous womb from a pregnant women before her unborn child is old enough to survive outside that womb. But this operation is not properly called abortion, nor need it be regarded as morally wrong. Here the death of the unborn is not the means to the benefit to the mother. This death is only an unavoidable side effect incidental to the life-saving operation.

The structure of this action, unlike the act of abortion, does not require one to intend the death of the child, and hence there is no turning against life even though destruction of life unavoidably occurs. (If, of course, those involved in such a procedure really do intend the death of the unborn child, as well as the saving of the mother's life, then the situation is radically different from the point of view of ethics and the action is morally wrong.)

Other examples

A man is walking down a dark street at night when a deranged-looking individual leaps out of the bushes, knife in hand, and attacks him. May he use force to resist such an attack? May he even kill the attacker? The answer: it depends. According to the principle we have been examining, the man is certainly justified in acting to preserve his life; in the situation described this is the good which he has pre-eminently in view. Since that is so, he can take action to preserve his life which also results in some harm to his attacker—provided there is no alternative open to him.

But is another course of action besides the use of force feasible? If such a practical course of action (for example, flight or evasion instead of force) does exist, then the ethically correct thing is to do that which will not involve harm to another good (in this instance, injury to the attacker). Supposing, however, that the only thing possible in the circumstances is to resist force with force, then the man should choose a form of resistance which involves no more force than is really necessary.

Suppose the individual who has been attacked is a policeman. He should, if possible, stun his attacker with his billy club rather than shoot him with his revolver; if it is necessary for him to use the revolver, he should shoot to wound his assailant rather than kill him; he should kill only if there is really nothing else to do.

Granted the artificiality of the example (few people, policemen or not, would be in a position in such circumstances to make the nice determinations and judgments just outlined), we are using it here to clarify a principle, not to describe the mental processes of an actual person in an actual situation. And the principle is this: if it is possible to realize the good one has in view without engaging in an ambiguous action which involves simultaneous harm to another good, one should do so; if such an ambiguous action is truly unavoidable, one should act in a way that will involve the least possible damage to the good which will be harmed.

It may be objected that in this case the good which is damaged is actually subordinated to the other good which is realized as a means to an end: the policeman clubs or shoots his assailant precisely in order to preserve his own life. Again, we can only say: it all depends. If this is the way the policeman regards his action, then, ethically speaking, that certainly is the way it is for him. But it is not necessary for him to analyze his action in this manner. He can correctly view injury to his assailant simply as the unavoidable consequence of the behavior required on his part to repel force and protect his life. Precisely how he regards the situation and his response to it is a question which only he—and perhaps not even he—can answer with certainty.

This, however, is not the same thing as saying that the morality of the action is determined by how the individual happens to regard it, as if one could make an intrinsically wrong act right simply by choosing to think of it as right. The point, rather, is that the structure of the action just described is such that it can legitimately and without doing violence to reality be seen as an act whose destructive aspect is not really a means to another good but rather an unavoidable consequence of the same act in which another good is realized.

The situation is quite different, however, in a different but not dissimilar case: capital punishment. Leaving aside rather nebulous and unconvincing arguments for capital punishment (e.g., the assertion that in cases where a life has been taken, another life must be destroyed in order to serve the imperatives of justice—which really comes down to little more than the morality of "an eye for an eye and a tooth for a tooth"), it seems clear that the only compelling consideration in favor of capital punishment is that it serves as a deterrent to would-be criminals.

There is some evidence that capital punishment actually does not deter crime. But supposing that the deterrent argument is factually valid, it still fails to constitute an ethical justification for capital punishment. Analysis of the action of capital punishment can only lead to the conclusion that a life is being taken precisely as a means to a remote good end: the deterrence of crime. (The same thing would apply to the argument that a particular person must be executed in order to prevent *him* from committing additional crimes in the future.) Since this is so, one must conclude that there is no ethical justification for capital punishment.

War

Finally, it may be helpful to apply what has been said to the difficult and controversial question of warfare, not in order to pronounce on the morality of any particular war but in order to illustrate the process by which an individual might make a judgment regarding his participation in war.

A great many requirements must be met before it is possible even to conclude that a military action has the quality of ambiguity discussed here. First, a military action cannot be morally acceptable if it is itself an implementation of an unjust policy or intention. Second, it cannot be justified if there are alternative ways, short of war, for protecting or realizing the goods which are at stake. Third, there must be solid reasons to believe that the military act has a chance of being effective, of realizing the goods at which it is directed: useless killing is always immoral. Fourth, inasmuch as war is a social act, it cannot be undertaken by the mere whim or private decision of any person—even of the highest public officials—but only in accord with the procedure authorized in a given society.

Finally, and assuming that these conditions are satisfactorily met (a very large assumption, incidentally, since they seldom are), there remains the question of how the individual soldier on the battlefield should behave and how he is to judge his action. May he or may he not kill an enemy soldier?

He can look on this action—the act of killing a member of the opposing military force in time of war—in either of two ways. He can see it as killing another human being as a means to an end—saving his own life, promoting the cause for which he is fighting, or whatever; or he can see it as an action which reduces by a certain amount the unjustly used force of the opposing side.

In the latter case he is not killing for the sake of killing—nor even killing for the sake of some other, presumably good end. Rather, he is performing an action directed to resisting and reducing unjust force, an action which unavoidably results in the injury or death of another person. As in the case of the policeman outlined above, it is not suggested that his feelings will necessarily correspond with this analysis of the action, but the question is not one of feelings but rather of the fundamental attitude according to which he views and engages in the act.

It should be emphasized that we are not making a defense of war. First, as we have said, the conditions which might justify a particular war are rarely satisfied in fact. Second, the requirements for an individual's participation in war—even assuming the war is not unjust as a whole—are not easily satisfied, are in fact generally ignored. But it is at least possible for an individual serving on the just side in a just war to carry out certain military duties in a morally right manner.

At this point it must be obvious why the problem of the ambiguous action is, from an ethical point of view, such a difficult one. Many different factors enter into the question: behavior, intention, close analysis of the total action in order to grasp its true structure. In real-life situations moral evaluation of such action can be difficult, even painful. The task, however, is one which no one concerned with judging and living in a morally responsible manner can avoid.

Up to this point we have elaborated an approach to ethics which does indeed make it possible to answer the question of whether an action is morally good or bad. But having an approach to ethics is by no means the same thing as incorporating that approach into one's own life or helping others incorporate it in theirs. In the chapters that follow we shall examine ways in which this can be done.

Questions for review and discussion

1. Does the discussion in the present chapter amount to a limitation or restriction of the eighth mode of responsibility?

2. Some people think the argument presented here gives up too

much—that it leads in fact to a position indistinguishable from utilitarianism. What is your opinion?

3. What difference does it make whether the good and bad aspects do or don't belong to one and the same indivisible action?

4. Can you think of examples of ambiguous acts which escape being wrong under the eighth mode of responsibility because of their ambiguity, but which nevertheless might be wrong under some other mode of responsibility?

5. Through the examples in this chapter an attempt is made to outline a consistent ethical position with regard to acts which threaten or destroy human life. Do you think the position is really consistent?

6. Some people have argued that one necessarily intends all the aspects and results of his action which he certainly foresees. Can you think of counterexamples to this contention?

7. At a number of points in the Bible, especially the Old Testament, God seems to be commanding someone to do something immoral. Assuming for the sake of argument that one takes these examples at their face value, is it possible to deal with the moral issue by using the theory of ambiguous action explained in this chapter?

8. Some argue that if war can ever be justified, the nuclear deterrent strategy intended to prevent war also can be justified. Do you agree?

9. If one who does his best to do what he thinks is right avoids moral guilt anyway, why bother to make a close analysis of ambiguous actions? Why not instead simply tell the individual to follow his conscience when the time comes?

15: Our Development as Persons Depends on Us

Shifting responsibility is a game everyone feels tempted to play on occasion. A person confronted with a difficult job almost instinctively takes a look around to see if he can find someone else to do the job for him. A person confronting the disastrous results of a job he has botched looks instinctively for someone or something else to blame for the catastrophe.

This built-in reluctance to accept responsibility is so much a part of fallible human nature that it comes as no surprise to find it operating in regard to the fundamental task of every person: determining what sort of person he will be. Each of us is responsible for his own development as a person, yet each of us is tempted to shift the responsibility elsewhere and to blame his failures on factors over which he has no control.

There is as a matter of fact good reason for doing so—up to a point. In many respects the development of a human being does depend upon factors beyond his control. These factors are of many different kinds, but basically they come down to two: heredity and environment, the inbred characteristics transmitted to an individual by his parents and previous generations of forebears and the circumstances of his life and the world in which he lives. Beyond doubt influences from these two sources do have a powerful impact in shaping and determining a human being. Beyond doubt, too, they are largely outside the control of the individual (although in the case of environment not always totally so).

But having said this, one has only stated the obvious without touching at all on the subject matter of ethics, the issue of freedom and its use. Granted that there are factors beyond our control which powerfully influence our development as human beings. But what of those factors which are *within* our power to control? There is the focal point of the challenge of freedom. And it is within this context that our development, not merely as human beings but rather as free, self-determining persons, must be worked out individually by each of us.

Our development as persons depends strictly on the way in which we use our freedom. And the use of freedom is not determined by heredity and environment, the factors over which we have no control. On the contrary, precisely to the degree that our choices and actions are determined by these factors, freedom does not enter into the picture at all.

It is true that for many individuals the area within which they are able to exercise freedom is drastically reduced and in the case of some (those suffering from severe mental illness, for example) diminished almost to the vanishing point. But again, having said this, one has really said very little. Whatever degree of freedom an individual possesses, whether great or small, his development as a person depends on the use he makes of that freedom.

If John is "very free" (has many possibilities open to him), he has a corresponding opportunity to develop as a person on a broad front. If Jane is "hardly free at all," her opportunity to develop as a person is correspondingly limited. But to whatever extent John and Jane and the rest of us enjoy freedom, to precisely that extent each of us is responsible for his individual development according to the manner in which he uses the freedom he has.

Ethics, in short, is not concerned with psychopathology or environmental limitations or with their consequences in human action. Psychopathology and environmental limitations are indeed facts of human life. But so is human freedom, and it is with freedom and its use that ethics is concerned.

An individual trying to live a morally good life may indeed find that factors over which he has no control interfere with his efforts. He may often find that he literally cannot do what he wishes he could do. But his development as a person does not depend upon that which he is truly unable to do (or, for that matter, unable to avoid doing) but rather on that which he is able to do (or avoid doing). His development as a person depends on what he does with his freedom.

Moral ideals

The most critical choice we make in life concerns the attitude we shall take toward moral ideals. It is critical because on it depends our attitude toward and exercise of our freedom. On this choice, in other words, depends all of our moral behavior, and thus our development as persons.

Moral standards are first presented to us in childhood—by parents, teachers, peers, a host of other persons and influences. Typically, the child accepts the moral standards on the basis of authority. His morality is a morality of obedience: to be obedient is to be morally good. With time and maturity, however, an individual outgrows the simple equation of morality and obedience. He is required then to take the stance which will govern his attitude toward moral ideals.

Two responses are possible. Aware perhaps that the moral standards which he learned as a child have their imperfections and limitations (may, in fact, be simply wrong), an individual can nevertheless adopt an attitude of willingness to submit himself and his life to moral standards—standards which may have been refined and perfected by comparison with those of childhood but which are real standards nevertheless.

Or, on the contrary, an individual can choose to regard moral standards—any possible standards, not just those of childhood—merely as facts with which he must contend as he goes about the business of getting what *he* wants out of life. A man can, in other words, choose to approach moral standards as the fundamental principles according to which he will seek to shape his life and himself, or he can regard them as external factors—no more important than many others—to be manipulated according to his own preferences and inclinations.

A man who takes this second attitude has quite simply rejected the task of developing as a person in favor of some more specific (and perhaps more immediately attractive) goal or combination of goals. He has equivalently elected not to shape his life by participating in fundamental goods constitutive of the human person; he has instead chosen a life radically limited to the pursuit of specific objectives.

In doing so he has also necessarily rejected genuine community, in which mutual acceptance and respect are based on the embodiment of fundamental goods in other persons, and has opted for what is at best a form of fragile coexistence with others which threatens to break down whenever he finds that the pursuit of his objectives is thwarted by another individual's pursuit of *his* goals.

If, by contrast, one chooses to submit himself to moral ideals, he has in fact committed himself to accept the responsibility of freedom. He has acknowledged that it is up to him to determine the person he will be and that this will come about by the use he makes of his freedom. In doing so he has not automatically become a complete person. But he has oriented himself in the direction—the only direction—which makes this possible.

Obviously the foregoing paragraphs suggest—as abstract presentations of living realities generally do—that the process by which an individual arrives at his stance toward moral ideals is a mechanical, cut-and-dried business. In fact, it is quite otherwise. The growing child, for example, does not normally face the question of moral standards as such and abstractly. The question, rather, is encountered in the concrete situations of daily life.

Faced with inner conflict—between the moral ideals that have been presented to him and the inclinations which tug at him to judge and act contrary to these standards—he gradually becomes aware that several quite different options are open to him. He may adhere to the standards he has received; he may seek for standards which are, perhaps, similar but at the same time sounder; or else he may act simply on the basis of his own desires and inclinations, without reference to any principle standing over against him in judgment.

Similarly, the adolescent (including the individual who is morally adolescent but may, chronologically, be well beyond adolescence) frames the problem for himself, not in terms of self-commitment and constitution, but rather in terms of authority and obedience and a clash between the two. Typically, the moral tension in his life is between doing as he pleases and doing as he has to do, and he thinks of what he "ought" to do as nothing more than one part—often a large and onerous part—of what he has to do.

Only gradually does he become able to remove the element of conflict and confrontation from his moral life and achieve for himself a stable reconciliation between those two poles—"what I want to do" and "what I have to do." Once an individual has reached this point, he has in effect reached moral maturity.

"Moral maturity" does not necessarily mean the same thing as "moral goodness." The morally mature person who is bad takes account of what he has to do but lives according to what he wants to do. The morally mature person who is good sees that moral standards represent the possibilities of his own life, the goods with which he can identify; he perceives that in acting for such goods his action is in fact true self-determination or self-constitution.

Even the morally mature good person, however, has not solved all his problems or reached a point at which his exercise of freedom of self-determination is easy and effortless. On the contrary, human freedom faces many obstacles—weakness, ignorance, the unsatisfactoriness of the concrete circumstances in which we find ourselves—and we must contend with these if we wish to become morally better than we are.

There is no magic formula for dealing with the factors which obstruct the exercise of our freedom, and the best advice is common-sense advice. Ignorance can be reduced by reflection and study concerning the factors involved in our lives, by seeking and listening to the advice and counsel of others, and by periodic self-examination. Weakness can be lessened by learning to control our emotions, not indeed by suppressing inclination but rather by using inclination to shape itself. For instance, if fear of the consequences of doing something that should be done inclines a person not to do it, he may find that attention to the good aspects of the matter—for example, the gratification he can expect from having done something which he considered right even though it was difficult—can stir up sufficient hope to overcome the fear.

The situation in which we find ourselves may often be beyond our power to control or alter significantly, but on the other hand it may at least be in our power to control the situation to some extent, and to control the way in which we expose ourselves to it (for example, a person struggling to cope with alcoholism might at least refrain from accompanying his heavy-drinking friends into a tavern). In short, while the exercise of such qualities as honesty, objectivity, and prudence will not remove all the things that stand in the way of the exercise of freedom, it will do away with at least some obstacles and help to render others more or less manageable.

Ultimately, our responsibility as free persons is both very simple and very difficult—simple to state and difficult (although immensely rewarding) to carry out. It comes down to this: to do the best we can to know what is right and the best we can to do it, refusing to give up in the face of our setbacks and failures, however serious and frequent they may be.

Questions for review and discussion

1. This chapter begins a new section of the book. Can you summarize what has been completed up to this point and what is now being undertaken?

2. We assume that heredity and environment can limit the possible exercise of freedom of self-determination. Identify some other ways in which limitations on freedom are sometimes formulated and expressed.

3. To what extent do you think you are free: in comparison with others of your own class and generation? in comparison with mem-

bers of a primitive tribe? in comparison with the poorest classes of our own society?

4. We describe in abstract language a fundamental option for or against moral ideals. Identify examples in fictional works in which such an option is being taken.

5. Is it in some sense a "reasonable" choice to choose against moral ideals? If so, is there any stronger reason for choosing in favor of them?

6. A person who makes a choice against moral ideals as the basis of his life is engaging in a third-level act which puts him into the framework of second-level action. He remains there unless he alters his fundamental option. To what purpose is such a person committing himself in his single, basic, third-level act?

7. It is frequently difficult for an adolescent to distinguish between the freedom of doing what you please and the freedom of self-determination. Why is this so?

8. We state that a person who makes a basic option on the side of moral ideals must still contend with ignorance, weakness, and unsatisfactory situations if he is to become morally better. Illustrate concretely what these obstacles are in some actual cases and discuss ways in which they might be overcome.

9. To what extent and in what ways do you think ignorance, weakness, and unfavorable situations can limit or even eliminate moral guilt?

10. Discuss the logic of a person who argues as follows: "Nobody's perfect anyway, so it isn't so bad if now and then I do something I admit to be immoral."

11. Is it possible for someone to be a subjectivist in ethical theory and consistently commit himself on the side of moral ideals?

16: Shaping the Future

"Give me a boy and I'll give you back a man." Social reformers, people bent on changing the world for the sake of a cause, almost always turn their sights eventually on children. The young represent the hope of the future. Not yet corrupted, not yet morally evil, they offer opportunity for a fresh start.

Their very receptiveness to external influences supports this view of children. Unlike adults, who seem relatively set in their ways, children can be shaped and changed, both intellectually and morally. In them seems to lie the hope of creating a world from which the failings and blemishes of the present have been eradicated. Thus the education of children is seen as the key to the future.

This view of education is plausible and by no means entirely mistaken. Education, broadly considered, can indeed play a powerful role in the formation of the young, including their moral development. But it is necessary to be realistic and not to overstate the case. The potential—of the child on one hand and any educational system on the other—is limited.

Specifically, it is not possible for any system of formation or education to *make* children morally good, since moral goodness (or badness) is a matter of *self-*determination.

An educational system can make it easier (or more difficult) for children to be morally good. It can create conditions under which the child, now and in the future, is more likely to choose rightly. But this is all it can do. There is no failure-proof formula for raising children in a way that will guarantee that they will be morally good adults, and, given the reality of what it means to be morally good, there can be none.

Not every educational theory recognizes that this is so. In fact, some notions about education proceed on the contrary assumption, that it is possible to make children morally good. In general, they do so because of mistaken ideas about morality itself. It is worth examining some of these theories briefly, both in order to see where they go wrong and also as a prelude to considering what can be accomplished through the education of children.

Commonplace at present, as well as at times in the past, is the idea that children are naturally good and therefore need only to be allowed to do as they please in order to grow up morally good persons. Immorality is seen as something that comes to them from the outside. But if they are permitted simply to follow their own instincts, they will inevitably do what is morally right.

This view of the matter would be correct if human beings were simply animals, since an animal which does what its instincts dictate is doing what is right for it as an animal. However, human beings are not simply animals, and human morality is a good deal more complex than that. Mere permissiveness does nothing to prepare a child for self-determination, which lies at the heart of adult morality. On the contrary, its likely result is to leave the child singularly ill-equipped to function in a genuinely self-determining manner in later life.

Another approach holds that moral evil is at bottom a matter of ignorance. Therefore, if the child is well informed—if he knows the facts—he will act intelligently and thus morally. One can agree that there is no value in having people misinformed and it is desirable that they be well informed. However, being well-informed is just not the same thing as being morally good. While ignorance is not a virtue, neither is knowledge.

People who are well-informed can put their knowledge to morally good uses—or to morally bad ones. A master criminal is not a morally good person simply because of his high intelligence and his command of a wide range of information. The Faust legend dramatizes the obvious fact that knowledge is one thing and moral goodness something else again.

Another theory holds that evil arises from society, from other people, and that children can therefore be protected from evil by being isolated from its carriers. There is certainly more than a grain of truth in this, and no sensible person wishes gratuitously to expose children to evil people.

At the same time, however, this view goes wrong when it identifies evil obsessively and almost exclusively with one group (the "communists" or the "capitalists," the "blacks" or the "whites," etc.) and concludes that segregating the child from the group thus identified as evil is a guarantee that the child himself will be good. Also, while it is reasonable to keep children from people who really are evil, this does not offer any ironclad assurance that they will exercise their own power of self-determination in a morally good way.

A fourth theory suggests that if people are compelled to act in ways that are good when they are young, they will as adults continue to do what is good. Simply put, this is a theory of good habits. But everything we have seen about moral maturity up to now underlines the fact that the moral goodness of an adult is not a matter of habit and routine but of correct, free, self-determining choice.

No doubt good habits are desirable, for both children and adults, and we may be morally responsible for bad habits we have. But good habits are not identical with good morality; indeed, an action performed simply out of habit (if there ever is such a thing) has no particular moral quality—good or bad—at all. The moral quality is in our efforts to keep or to alter our habits.

Each of these educational/formational theories goes wrong in ignoring the fact that moral goodness and moral evil result from self-determination. Moral goodness cannot be guaranteed or moral evil eradicated by education. Human beings retain the power to dispose of their own lives, for good or ill, regardless of the educational system to which they have been exposed. And to the extent that education might deprive an individual of the capacity for self-determination, it would also drain his life of moral quality.

Even if the science-fiction dream of some determinists were realized—a system of education which would condition individuals always to do what is right—the result would be far removed from a situation in which everyone was, in the full sense of the words, "morally good." In such circumstances people's actions would have no more moral quality—good or bad—than the behavior of obedient animals or well-programmed machines. (The recalcitrant persistence of human freedom, however, suggests that no such system is likely soon to become reality.)

What education can do

Having seen what education *cannot* accomplish as far as morality is concerned, it is time now to turn to the more important question of what it can do. For if education cannot guarantee morally good behavior, in either the child or the adult, it can at least make it easier for child and adult to choose and do what is morally right. It can do this in several ways.

First, education must recognize in confronting a child that, in regard to morality as well as other matters, he *is* a child and not a miniature adult. It is a mistake to suppose that a young child is capable of self-determination in the same way as a morally mature adult.

Although the child does make choices in a sense, he is not aware of himself as self-determining and is therefore incapable of full self-determination. Morally speaking, he is at a stage where obedience (or its contrary) is the dominant factor, and necessarily so. Thus it is essential that sound rules be formulated and enforced to govern the behavior of children. No one responsible for their education should have to apologize for doing so.

At the same time, however, rules for children must meet various criteria. They should be consistent, since otherwise they embody some irrationality and cannot really be followed. Like any good system of law, the rules should also be clear, since otherwise the child cannot tell what is expected of him (and cannot in fairness be punished for failing to do it). The rules, furthermore, should be non-exploitative.

Too many rule-systems for children are, in fact, designed for the benefit of adults—parents or teachers—and are not really in the best interests of the children at all. Ideally, a set of nonexploitative moral rules for children will be made up of rules which children would set for themselves if they were able—if, that is, they were fully self-determining and bent on doing what is morally right.

If the rule-system is developed in this way, it will be possible for the individual, as he matures, to incorporate essentially the same rules—albeit, in many cases, more sophisticated versions—into his life. Thus, instead of having to make a sharp transition from childhood morality to adult morality, the individual will experience his moral life as a continuum in which he achieves deeper insight into moral principles rather than abandoning old principles in favor of new ones.

At the same time, while providing moral rules for the child, an educational system must take care not to over-organize his life. It is extremely important that there be free areas dispersed throughout his day in which, acting within the general framework of the rules, he is nevertheless free to investigate and experiment in making choices for himself among various goods.

It is a mistake for parents and teachers rigidly to plan and organize all of the child's time for him, even though they may be tempted to do this "for his own good." Children need opportunity for free and spontaneous activity, within a system of rules, and this is extremely important to their moral development.

During free areas which he shares with adults the child is introduced—noncoercively—to goods to which it is worthwhile to commit himself. He is given the opportunity of sharing in the committed activity of adults engaged in doing something which is valuable for its own sake.

This is not simply a matter of togetherness or even of adults giving good example to children. The point, rather, is that the child learns what commitment to human goods

means by seeing adults performing actions which express
their commitment and by having opportunity to share in
such activity (without, however, being pressured to do so).
Thus, a simple family outing during which the parents
genuinely relax and enjoy themselves and the children are
invited to share in the enjoyment can teach children much
more than any amount of words what "participation" in
the good of play is really all about.

Equally important are the free areas which the child
shares with other children, which in our society are generally grouped under the label of "playing." A child's play
may seem a more or less meaningless activity to an adult,
but it has a crucial role in the child's moral development.
In play situations with other children the child develops a
sense of fairness and justice and comes to appreciate the
necessity for authority within relationships which are non-
exploitative and nonpaternalistic.

Finally, the child needs free areas by himself—periods in
which he has opportunity to reflect, dream, and seek
himself in forms of activity in which he engages for no
other reason except that he enjoys and values them. Such
periods are, in effect, occasions to prepare for and rehearse
the acts of self-determination by which he will constitute
himself as a person.

One of the much debated questions about the raising of
children is whether and when to use force. Force must
sometimes be employed to prevent the child from doing
what is wrong. Force intended to compel a child to do
what is right is, at best, meaningless as far as any contribution to moral maturity is concerned. For in terms of moral
maturity it is only the good which one elects to do—not
the good which one is compelled to do—which has value.

Forcing a child to do good things can actually have
negative results in the long run. The child who is coerced
to spend half an hour a day practicing the piano may very

well grow up with an aversion to music; it is much more likely that the child who has been encouraged but not compelled to take pleasure in music will grow up as an adult capable of freely appreciating the good of which music is an expression.

In short, moral rules and the enforcement of those rules for children should be mainly negative: directed at preventing the child from doing what is wrong rather than compelling him to do what is right. Good done as a result of compulsion provides at best a shaky foundation for later virtue.

The moral development of the child also requires that his emotions be educated. It is extremely important that he be helped to develop hope—an attitude based on belief that things which are hard but worthwhile can be accomplished. This can be done by encouraging the child to undertake tasks which are difficult but possible.

If things are always too easy for the child, he has no need to hope, and he will be unprepared for later challenges which are not easy at all. If, on the other hand, things are too difficult for him—if he is consistently frustrated by failing at the tasks which are set for him—he is likely to conclude that no amount of effort is ever likely to produce good results and to adopt an attitude of despair.

Furthermore, it is wise to encourage the child to strive for goals in areas he is interested in (sports, hobbies, etc.) even if these seem, by adult standards, frivolous and trivial. So far as moral development is concerned, what is at stake is the maturing of a particular attitude rather than the acquisition of useful skills or social graces.

The child should also be helped to develop self-control. This is done, not by threats and punishment, but rather by proposing a self-ideal for him: "Isn't this what you really want to do and to be? Then in order to accomplish it, this is what you must do." Successes in conforming to the self-ideal proposed are praised and rewarded. Thus the child is given support and encouragement in overcoming emotional barriers and fitting his actions to the self-ideal.

As the child's ability to understand grows, he must be given reasons for the moral rules which have been set for him. The reasons given should be the real ones—framed, of course, in concepts and language he is able to grasp. The child should also be included in the process by which important family decisions are reached. The making of the decisions should not be turned over to him, but he should be exposed to the process by which adults arrive maturely at important decisions and allowed, to the extent of his growing competence, to contribute to the deliberative process.

It is also important that the child have companions who share the same moral framework and outlook on life as he. This does not mean he should be segregated from children who reflect other viewpoints—something which would be impossible even if it were hypothetically desirable. It does mean that he should have an opportunity to be part of a community of children whose value-system is the same and who, within the framework of that value-system, can proceed autonomously to develop their own rules and structures.

Providing such a setting for children is relatively easy in large families, where brothers and sisters tend to create a community together. It is more difficult today, when families are smaller and neighborhoods are usually quite heterogeneous, and it may therefore take special effort and ingenuity on the part of parents to see to it that children do in fact have this opportunity of associating with other children who share the same moral standards. The effort is, however, well worth making because of the importance of this factor in moral development.

Finally, a word about religious training. It is a mistake to suppose that one can make a child good by making him religious, and the mistake lies basically in the fact that this degrades religion by making it an instrument of morality. This is reflected in the attitude of parents who say they "send Johnny to Sunday school to be sure he gets some moral training." Religion should be presented to children as something valid and valuable in itself, not as an adjunct of good moral behavior.

It is true that most religious systems do demand a moral commitment on the part of the individual believer. But in this case the individual wants, presumably, to behave in a morally correct manner because of his religious beliefs; he seeks to be moral because he wants to be holy rather than the other way around.

The ideal of sanctity (as a function of religion) can indeed be a powerful inducement to moral behavior on the part of one who accepts the ideal. But neither holiness nor ethical goodness is likely to be served by confusing the two things and attempting to use religion (or religious training) as a means to induce good behavior on the part of the child.

Nor can religious training be merely a matter of brainwashing and indoctrination. Rather, religion—grounded ultimately on convictions about the reality of a transcendent Other with whom (or which) it is important to be in a proper relationship—should be presented to the child as an alternative to the worldview of egoism, in which the rest of the world is seen as revolving around oneself. Religious transcendence does have powerful ethical implications, reinforcing and validating as it does the willingness of an individual to submit himself to values and standards beyond himself.

This view of religion, however, is scarcely likely to come across to the child in a setting in which religion itself is reduced to the role of a mere handmaid of good moral behavior.

We cannot end this part of our exposition without pointing out that the suggestions we have put forth (like the suggestions of others) do not guarantee the moral progress of individuals and society as a whole. There can be no such guarantees as long as human freedom remains a reality. We shall examine what this means in greater detail in the chapter which follows.

Questions for review and discussion

1. Think of examples from your experience of educational practices which seemed to be based on the various theories of education mentioned near the beginning of this chapter. How in your opinion did these practices work out?

2. Can you think of reasons why so many approaches to education seem to be based on denial—at least in practice—of freedom of self-determination?

3. The theories of education which we reject are not normally presented as alternatives to a philosophy of education based on freedom of self-determination. Research educational theory a bit and see how such theories actually are presented.

4. As long as substantive human goods are actually realized, does it really make any difference whether or not action is done by freedom of self-determination? If so, what difference?

5. Think of examples of rules made by adults to govern the behavior of children. Criticize these examples according to the criteria suggested.

6. In what sense of "freedom" are the free areas of a child's life free?

7. Do you think the lives of most children today are over-organized? What do you think of the fact that many children spend a great part of their free time watching television?

8. In relationships of adults with children what subtle forms of force are often employed to try to compel them to do what is good?

9. Gather information about institutions for delinquent children. To what extent are such institutions likely to cultivate an attitude of hope? How could they do so?

10. How does the proposal that children be assured companions who share the same value framework differ from a proposal to practice segregation?

11. If you have experienced religious education, discuss the extent to which it may have confused the religious with the ethical.

12. Show how the theory of education proposed in the present chapter is based on considerations in chapter fifteen.

17: Progress in Perspective

Back in the 1920s a popular charlatan encouraged people to psych themselves by repeating regularly, "Every day in every way I'm getting better and better." Foolish as the phrase sounds now, it epitomizes an enduring phenomenon—the notion that human progress is continuous and inevitable.

The idea that progress is inevitable has taken form in many different ways throughout history. Two of these are important in the contemporary world: Marxism and a vulgarized version of evolutionary theory.

Adopting a pseudoscientific approach, the dialectical view of history espoused by orthodox Marxists attempts to lay down firm predictions regarding the historical process. The difficulty is that such predictions concerning the inevitable march of events have not been borne out by the facts. This point has been discussed at length by critics of Marxism, and there is no need to repeat at length here what has been said elsewhere. It is simply a fact that history has not turned out the way it should according to the dialectic of Marx and Engels. Reality has proved to be more complicated than the inevitable pattern of developments they envisioned.

As far as evolutionary theory is concerned, it is necessary to distinguish between biological evolutionism and evolution loosely conceived as an optimistic philosophy of progress. As a biological hypothesis accounting for the variety of types of organic life, evolutionary theory makes no pretense of guaranteeing inevitable progress. The process of selection merely determines that some kinds of life will survive and others will die off, not that this will necessarily represent qualitative advancement. One can easily imagine a state of affairs in which man could no longer survive on the earth but in which insects continued to survive and flourish. The cockroach, in that case, could be the "highest" form of life.

Nevertheless, some philosophers, notably Herbert Spencer in the nineteenth century, attempted to translate evolutionism into a comprehensive theory of progress. Spencer was hailed in his day as a great thinker, but little is heard of him now. The reason is obvious. The First and Second World Wars, the Great Depression, Auschwitz, the Stalinist terror, Hiroshima and Nagasaki, Vietnam—these and many other vast calamities of the twentieth century have made it all but impossible for intelligent people to swallow the idea that the progress of the human race in history is in any way guaranteed.

Indeed, the overriding fact of contemporary history is that the human race, far from having moved steadily forward, now confronts the appalling possibility of wiping itself off the face of the earth. This is not what most people mean by progress.

Is progress possible?

On the other hand, it is clear enough that mankind has indeed made real progress in many fields over the centuries. Progress is apparent in such areas as theoretical knowledge and technology. Indeed, it is only in virtue of progress in these areas that man now has the capability of destroying himself. But the progress involved here might more correctly be described as "accumulation." In mathematics, for example, a reasonably apt student can now accomplish things far beyond what Euclid was capable of. Mathematicians now know more than Euclid did and are therefore able to do more than he could do. This truly is progress of a sort.

Progress exists in philosophy, too. Not that the basic philosophical problems have been finally resolved or are likely to be. Rather, what has happened over the course of centuries is that certain solutions have come to be seen as unacceptable. At least the philosopher now knows that some answers to some questions, which at one time seemed plausible to reasonable people, are simply invalid and untenable. This also represents progress.

Technological progress is an overwhelming fact of life today. There was, after all, a time in the history of the race when people did not know the use of the wheel and of fire. Now man travels to the moon and splits the atom as a source of energy.

Similarly, there is a kind of progress in the fine arts. This is not to say that Picasso is a greater painter than Botticelli, or Stravinsky a finer composer than Bach. But the painter today commands certain techniques—methods of pigmentation and perspective, for instance—which were unknown to painters a thousand years ago; today's musician has a far wider range of sounds at his disposal, thanks to the development of modern instruments and electronic devices, than the Renaissance composer did. As a result of improved technique, today's painter and composer can *do* things which painters and composers of earlier centuries could not do. Moreover, apart from accidental losses, the creative accomplishments of previous ages remain available for us to admire and, if we wish, to imitate, while our artists go on in an attempt to set new standards of creativity. While much of what they do will fall away, some of it will become part of the cultural heritage of later generations.

This list can be extended. Men and women today—at least in some countries of the world—are physically larger and stronger than their ancestors, enjoy better health, and live longer. They have more leisure and also have greater access to resources for play, aesthetic experience, and intellectual pursuits. All this, too, represents progress.

But the progress involved is essentially one of accumulation. People are able to do more—to realize certain goods more fully. This, however, does not imply that they live morally better lives. The accumulation of skills and techniques, of tools and technologies, make it theoretically possible for people to do more moral good; but it makes it just as possible for them to do more moral evil.

In short, the kind of "progress" achieved by the human race up to now offers no grounds for assuming the inevitability of moral progress. It only means that over the centuries there has been an expansion of human ability to do both good and evil.

This has not always been clear to modern thinkers and is not clear to all of them today. More than fifty years ago John Dewey, noting the fact of technological progress, complained that the social sciences had lagged behind the natural sciences and suggested that something could and should be done about this. Dewey believed that the moral dimension of human life should be susceptible to external control, more or less as technology had been brought to bear in the solution of physical problems. For example, supposing we fully understood the causes of crime, it ought to be possible to devise and apply techniques which would eradicate or at least effectively control the criminal propensities in men.

The difficulty with this view, however, is that it fails to recognize the radical difference between human action and technique. Techniques aim to achieve specific, concrete objectives; they fail only by error or accident. But human action as such—that is, action which is free—aims at open-ended ideals and fails precisely because of a failure of choice; because, that is, a person chooses to settle for limited goals and, in doing so, closes himself off from other possibilities whose realization would make him more fully human.

Suppose for a moment the hypothetical possibility of devising a human technology which would indeed some-how make it impossible to make morally evil choices. Denied the opportunity of choosing wrongly, we would in fact be denied the opportunity of choosing freely. And in the absence of freedom human life would no longer have any moral quality. Because action was no longer free, it would be neither morally good nor morally bad.

A human technology (some kind of super psychic conditioning or brainwashing, for instance) might—again hypothetically—eliminate moral evil from human life, but it would do so at the cost of simultaneously eliminating moral goodness. It would achieve its end by reducing the person to the status of an object, to be manipulated by "experts," persons of presumably superior and virtually superhuman wisdom and moral rectitude.

The only conclusion from all this is that, as far as morality is concerned, there is no such thing as necessary and inevitable progress. As long as man is free, and to the extent that he is free, he retains a dual capacity for moral good and moral evil. He is able to choose well or badly. Only by eliminating his freedom could one eliminate the possibility of his choosing evil; in the process one would also eliminate the possibility of his freely choosing good.

This is not a pessimistic view of man. It does not say that human life goes around in circles or that each generation is condemned to repeat mistakes of previous generations. But neither does it say that the course of history is necessarily forward and upward. Rather, the pattern of human history presents a broken front: some progress in some areas at some times, together with regression in other areas at the same time. Such a view is neither pessimistic nor optimistic; it is simply realistic.

It may be objected that in our times there are signs that the human race is indeed capable not simply of spotty and uncertain moral progress but of genuine moral breakthroughs. The weakening of nationalism—which has been the cause of so much conflict and suffering in history—is cited as one example. So is the disappearance in most places of slavery.

Yet the decline of nationalism can be seen as a mere by-product of improvement in communications techniques and the development of new technology drawing the peoples of the world more closely together. The virtual disappearance of slavery can be attributed to the fact that slavery is only economically practical in agricultural societies, whereas modern societies are increasingly industrialized.

In short, these and other developments in our times do not reflect steadily evolving moral progress but point only to the fact that archaic practices (and abuses) are generally discontinued as they become less useful. Furthermore, without belaboring the point, it is difficult to make a

compelling argument for steady and inevitable moral progress in the age of Auschwitz, the nuclear deterrent, and
widespread abortion-on-request.

The search for panaceas

Confronting the fact that a realistic view of history and
the human condition gives no ground for optimism about
the inevitability of moral progress, men at various times
have come up with panaceas intended to remove the obstacles to such progress and insure it in the future. We will
take note of four here: the psychoanalytic panacea, the
new morality panacea, the panacea of new institutions and
new communities, and the religious panacea.

The psychoanalytic panacea (a complex of psychological and sociological notions based loosely on the theories of Freud and others) reduces evil to illness. Men have
hang-ups—mental and emotional quirks—which cause them
to act badly. If they can be cured of these, and if techniques of child-raising and education can be devised which
prevent their recurrence in future generations, the cause of
evil will be eliminated and men will be good.

It is true that emotional illness is a reality, and it is true
that some emotional illnesses can be cured or at least
alleviated by psychoanalysis or other forms of therapy.
But it is not true that if men are released from their
psychic hang-ups, they will then necessarily do what is
right. On the contrary, if a man is really made more free
by therapy, his capacity for free choice—of evil as well as
good—is thereby increased. Curing an individual of his
neurosis may make him healthy, but it does not guarantee
that he will be morally good.

The new-morality approach stresses the idea that the old
morality kept man in bondage and made him a hypocrite.
Now, however, we are to enjoy a morality of freedom.
Man has come of age, and he will henceforth act maturely

and responsibly. The treatment in the preceding chapters of the responsibilities of freedom indicates the extent to which there is something valid in the claims of the new morality, but we are also in a position to see that freedom to do as one pleases is not the same as freedom of self-determination.

Unfortunately for the high hopes placed by some in the new morality, new moralities have come along with depressing regularity over the centuries, always making the same claims to liberate man and usher in a new age. It has not happened yet, and on the evidence there is no reason to suppose that it will happen in the future.

The panacea of institutional reform attributes evil to institutions, which are said to distort and corrupt human relationships. Change—or perhaps do away with—institutions, create new communities, adopt new patterns of human relationship, and men will cease to do evil and become universally good and loving and generous. As we have seen, large societies always are a mixture of community and exploitation; perhaps small communes based on immediate interpersonal relationship—and excluding anyone over thirty—will do better.

While it is true that many institutions are corrupt and all of them imperfect, the evidence of history shows, once again, that it is naive to expect much in this direction. Movements of institutional reform (or revolution) have recurred repeatedly and, just as repeatedly, have failed to bring about the promised golden age. Indeed, the evidence suggests that it is generally wiser to attempt to build on the basis of whatever community exists within present institutions instead of tearing down existing institutions and communities in the hope that what comes after will somehow be better than what went before. The average life expectancy of a commune, we are told, is a couple of months.

The religious panacea, finally, comes in two forms: on the one hand, the religion or religions we have had up to now have failed us and we therefore must have a new religion; on the other, all religion is a snare and a delusion, distracting man from his proper area of concern in this world and placing him in thrall to myths and to a priestly caste bent on perpetuating those myths—and so, for man to be freed from superstition in order to pursue his proper destiny, religion itself must be done away with.

Each of these pseudosolutions to the problem of human happiness and goodness has enjoyed popularity at various times in history, and both have a certain vogue at the present moment. Yet neither solution has up to now contributed anything very tangible to the improvement of human life, and taken together they simply cancel each other out. Partisans of religion may look back to the "age of faith" as a high-point in human history, conveniently forgetting the Inquisition and the wars of religion; partisans of modern secularism may bask in the glow of the "enlightenment," conveniently forgetting that totalitarian ideologies have replaced ancient theologies and that the earthly paradise of unlimited consumption has brought the world's wealthiest nation to the point where it is smothering under its own garbage.

At bottom, all of these panaceas are based on the conviction that man is not really free and that, therefore, the source of human moral goodness and moral evil lies outside man's self-determination. Yet the thrust of everything we have said up to now comes down to this: man is free, man is self-determining, and man makes himself good or evil according to his own free choice. If that is so, there is and can be no such thing as inevitable moral progress on the part of the human race.

Progress is possible for us—individually and together—if we choose it. But to say it is possible for us to make moral progress is not at all the same as saying that it is inevitable that we will make progress. We are free to choose well, to make choices by which we realize more fully what it means to be human. But because we are free, we can also choose badly, opting if we wish for growing depersonalization and inhumanity. There is no inevitability here; in a true and profound sense it is up to us to make of ourselves, individually and together, what we choose to be.

Questions for review and discussion

1. We deal here only in passing with Marxism. Investigate other aspects of this philosophy as a theory of progress. Consider other criticisms proposed against the philosophy and also other aspects of Marxism which make it as attractive as it obviously is to many people.

2. In what sense does biological evolution guarantee the "survival of the fittest"? To what extent does the concept of evolution change as it is applied in other areas of the natural sciences—e.g., the evolution of the physical universe? To the social sciences—e.g., cultural evolution?

3. Has progress in science and technology been constant throughout history? How can it be accounted for?

4. To what extent would a morally good person be intent upon furthering progress in the areas in which progress is possible?

5. Explain the relationship between Dewey's attitude toward progress and his theory of situationism, discussed in chapter ten.

6. Do you know of any theories in psychology that propose to produce good men by a process of human engineering?

7. List present-day phenomena that might be used to argue either for or against the occurrence of moral progress. Apart from the theoretical consideration that man has freedom of self-determination, do you see any strong reasons for arguing either for or against the proposition that moral progress occurs?

8. Do you know of—or can you find examples of—the positions on progress we regard here as panaceas? What is there about each of these positions that makes it plausible to intelligent people?

9. Any theory which holds moral progress to be inevitable excludes freedom of self-determination. But proponents of such theories often argue that the end of progress will be precisely freedom, or increasing freedom. "Freedom" in what sense or senses?

18: Revolution and Reform

Closely linked to the question of whether and how moral progress is possible is what role, if any, revolution and reform can play in making human society more just and more virtuous. The issue is particularly pressing today when revolution is frequently proclaimed as not only a solution but the *only* solution to evil and injustice in society.

The problem is a complicated one. There are three quite different kinds of relationship among people—exploitative, contractual, and communitarian—and all three are generally found intertwined in any large and complex society. Since the relationships are different, the remedies to abuses will also be different; yet because the relationships coexist in the same society, a solution which from one perspective might be appropriate to correct an abuse may, considered in the light of a different form of relationship, be inappropriate and even harmful.

Thus, while violent revolution may be urged as the proper solution to abuses of an exploitative nature, it must also be recognized that revolution is likely to destroy whatever elements of community exist within a society. It is not easy fo answer the question of how to proceed in such circumstances.

As in the case of individual evil, various false or at best partial solutions are proposed to the problem of evil in society. On the analogy that society is an organism, social evil is explained as a sort of disease, a form of social pathology. Or evil is ascribed to lack of communication; presumably, if people and groups communicate more freely and fully with one another, social evils will vanish. Another theory attributes the evil that exists in society to a particular class or group: the capitalists or the communists, the Blacks or the whites, the rebellious young or the hypocritical middle-aged, and so forth. In still another view social evil is the fruit of bad institutions—institutions which are too large and impersonal; salvation is seen to lie in small groups—various types of mini-society.

Each of these explanations of evil in society locates its cause elsewhere than in self-determination. But, as we have stressed repeatedly, *moral* evil is precisely the result of self-determination. Undoubtedly societies suffer from other ills than those which can be described as moral ones, and to the extent that this may be true in a given society each of the explanations of evil noted above may have some validity. But to the extent that the evil in society is moral evil no explanation or solution is realistic which fails to see that moral evil is rooted in self-determination. And explanations that are unrealistic in this matter will be unlikely to contribute to the eradication of social evil even to the extent that it may be due to factors other than the moral one.

The only remedy for the abuse of human freedom is the proper use of freedom. Failure to acknowledge either that freedom exists or that it is sometimes abused leads only to a dead-end street as far as correcting moral evil—in society as well as in the individual—is concerned.

Social relationships

The problems—and remedies—in each of the three kinds of social relationship are different. We shall look briefly at each to see what avenues of redress are open to those suffering as a result of someone else's misuse of freedom.

If the relationship is exploitative, the obvious course of action for those who are exploited is to gain enough power to change the relationship to a contractual one, in which both sides (or all sides) derive roughly equal benefits. If the exploitation exists within a larger society where there is a common authority, the exploited can appeal to that authority to correct the abuse and right the balance. (In the United States, for instance, this presumably is one of the crucial functions of a body such as the Supreme Court.) Finally, as a last resort, the exploited individual or group can employ physical force in an effort to halt the exploitation. Realistically, however, this is not likely to be successful if the exploiter has made an accurate calculation of the relative power (and potential power) available to himself and to the exploited.

If physical violence is used, it is equivalently warfare, and the same stringent limitations on the use of force in war which were noted earlier must be observed. Rebellion can only be justified as warfare is. Furthermore, it should be clear that this is not revolution in the same sense in which that word is often used in the contemporary world. Modern prophets of revolution give the term an almost mystical meaning, using it to describe some sort of fundamental transformation in man. But revolution—the use of physical force—intended simply to end an exploitative relationship does not involve any such fundamental transformation; it is merely the direct use of force being used to counter unjust force being used for exploitation.

A contractual relationship is midway between exploitation and community. It is a kind of mutual exploitation: each party gives up something to the other (or others) in order that he may get something in return. In a fair contractual relationship that which each surrenders is roughly comparable in value to that which he receives. However, an initially just contractual relationship can degenerate into a sort of sanctioned exploitation when one of the parties begins giving less and getting more.

This can happen in either of two ways: either one of the parties more or less deliberately violates the terms of the contract or else the conditions to which the contract applies change significantly, so that the balance shifts and one party finds himself having to give a great deal and receive very little while the other gives very little and receives a great deal. When a contractual relationship changes in this way, it has in fact ceased to be a contract and has become ordinary exploitation instead.

That being so, the means of redress are those outlined above when exploitation occurs: appeal by the injured party to the sense of justice of the exploiting party, appeal to an authority having power to enforce contracts, and—in extreme cases—recourse to violence in order to counter the violence of the exploiter. The moral difficulty with resort to violence is that there often is no act that the exploited party can do that will in and of itself lessen the violence being done to him; violence, therefore, is likely to be a means to an ulterior end, and morally excluded for that reason.

Of course, when a contract is violated by one party, the injured party no longer is morally obliged to observe its terms, but often this is of little help. Either the injured party has already carried out his part of the contractual arrangement or in many cases he can be made to suffer more loss than gain if he does not carry through his part of the arrangement, even though it is not just that he should have to do so.

On the other hand, there is reason to think that it is generally less difficult to correct exploitation resulting from a contractual relationship which has gone sour than it is to correct an exploitative situation which never involved anything else except exploitation. At least in the case of what started out as a contract there was an initial commitment on both sides to a rough kind of equity, and if this commitment has not vanished entirely it may be possible to reconstruct the relationship on its basis.

At the same time, however, contract is a more impersonal kind of relationship than either direct exploitation or community. As such, it is possible for a contractual relationship to become exploitative without ill will on anyone's part, simply as a result of changed circumstances which no one anticipated or particularly intended.

This suggests that in a concrete situation of mixed exploitation and community it may not be advisable to attempt to change the relationship to a purely contractual one. In particular cases it may be better to seek to correct the situation by building on such elements of community as already exist rather than eliminating community along with exploitation by making the relationship exclusively contractual.

For example, the solution to the problems of a family in which the parents, although basically loving, are habitually exploitative of their children might better be sought in counseling, encouragement, and mutual efforts at understanding and charity than in legal action, which might end in separating the parents from their children and making them wards of the state.

Communities, as we have seen, are based on a shared

commitment by their members to the mutual realization of some fundamental good or goods. Communities can go wrong in their constituting act (the original Constitution of the United States, for example, made provision for slavery), in the institutions which express constitutional purposes, or in particular actions. The institutions of a community are corrupt when, either as a result of design or accident, they embody exploitation.

Tax loopholes which unjustly favor some individuals or groups at the expense of others are a good example of this; in some cases tax breaks may originally have had a justification, but over a period of time they have become simply means by which some members of the community are required to pay for the special privileges which others enjoy; in other cases the loopholes may have been unjust from the start—they were never anything but a kind of institutionalized exploitation hiding behind the facade of law.

Finally the injustice which exists in communities as a result of particular actions comes about when individuals fail to carry out the duties which are properly theirs by reason of their roles in society. As we have seen, an individual faced with a genuine conflict of duties may be morally excused from performing some of them. But an individual cannot consistently claim the benefits which come from membership in particular societies and neglect the duties that arise from such membership without being guilty of injustice and irresponsibility.

Reform of community

Because a community is what it is, the only way to correct evil compatible with the principle of community is communication, persuasion, an appeal to reason and good will (not excluding an appeal to emotion). Community can never be protected by force, because the use of force by some members of the community against others is inherently destructive of community.

If, then, individuals in a community are guilty of evil actions, one must appeal to the institutions that embody the community's purposes in an effort to persuade such individuals to live up to the duties which those institutions impose. If the institutions embody evil and injustice, one must appeal to the constitutional principles of the community in order to have the institutions brought into conformity with those purposes.

It is of course possible to use force at the operational level and it may even be necessary at times to do so (for instance, people who break the law must sometimes be arrested and imprisoned), and at the institutional level it is also possible to play politics in an effort to achieve an advantageous result without correcting what is wrong in the institutions. But to the extent that either of these things is done, the principle of community has been abandoned and the relationship has been forced into the pattern of either exploitation or contract.

Where problems within a community relate to fundamental constitutional principles, the methods of tackling the difficulty must be essentially philosophic. One may, for example, attempt to demonstrate to other members of the community that a particular part of the constitution is inconsistent with other principles embodied there: for instance, toleration of slavery cannot very well coexist with commitment to the principle that human beings are fundamentally equal and possess equal rights.

If, however, there is no demonstrable inconsistency and the constituting principles are in fact mutually consistent, the only recourse is an appeal to basic principles of right and wrong which should govern action independently of any other commitments. Admittedly the chances of success in such circumstances are not great. When the members of a community are bent on doing what is wrong, arguments intended to point out to them that there are other values they ought not violate are not likely to be heeded.

It is essential in any case that when something goes wrong in a community relationship, one who would seek to set it right proceed on the assumption that the other members of the community are acting with good will. If one starts with the opposite assumption—of ill will—one has already undercut the very possibility of community.

Furthermore, in some cases it may be better to maintain an imperfect community—such as the sort of unhappy but tolerable family situation described above—than to transform the entire relationship into a contractual one. A community, even an imperfect one, at least contains the seeds of growth in personal relationship, whereas a contract is altogether impersonal.

There can never be community between those who do violence and those who have violence done to them, at least not while the violence is occurring. Community depends on mutual self-commitment, and there is no sharing among people who do violence to each other. To be sure, it may be justifiable to resort to violence in some complex communities—for example, to overthrow an oppressive dictator. In such cases those who employ violence are obviously not maintaining community with the individual or group against whom the violence is directed, but it may be that the use of violence is the only way of preserving the possibility of community for everyone else.

Such cases are rare, however. And—other things being equal—the larger the group to whom violence is done, the less likely it is that the violence is justifiable (at least, as an instrument for preserving community).

In practical terms this suggests that the smaller the

number of revolutionaries in a given society is in relation to the society as a whole, the more likely it is that the revolutionaries are in fact would-be tyrants, obsessed perhaps with some scheme for transforming human nature by means which invariably turn out to be violent and exploitative. Whatever their rhetoric may assert, such people do not really have community in view, but are only bent on imposing their vision of how people should live and society should function on everybody else.

Social change brought about by violence will be no more stable than the ability of those who employed the violence to remain in power. As long as they have not received the consent of those they govern, they are only exercising a kind of tyranny. At best, such a situation may represent a kind of contractual relationship and can in particular cases be an improvement over a previously existing situation of exploitation. But it is far removed from community, and it may retard rather than advance the attainment of a truly communitarian relationship among persons.

Questions for review and discussion

1. To what extent do you think the ills of society arise from moral evil and to what extent from other causes?

2. In practice how are the exploitative, the contractual, and the communitarian aspects of a society to be distinguished, when in fact they are mixed in the same social situation?

3. Can you think of historical cases in which a nonideological rebellion of a genuinely exploited group of people succeeded in changing the situation of exploitation? How did the exploiters come to miscalculate?

4. We speak of a contractual relationship as midway between exploitation and community. This is an oversimplified, shorthand way of putting the matter. Can you think of more refined ways of defining the similarities and differences of the various forms of relationship?

5. It has been said that in the United States there is a tendency

for every great social issue sooner or later to come before the Supreme Court. Can you explain this in terms of the analysis offered in this chapter?

6. Existing ways of treating criminals apparently tend to alienate them still further from society. But some proposals for reform are based on at least implicit denial of freedom of self-determination. Assuming freedom of self-determination, is there any way to deal with a criminal which would be better than present methods?

7. In this chapter we take a rather dim view of revolution, especially revolution on ideological grounds. Does this mean that our position is committed to a conservative or status quo stance on issues involving social justice?

8. For lack of space, the brief treatment offered here does not go into a number of important questions, such as civil disobedience. Investigate what is involved in civil disobedience and other tactics of confrontation politics and discuss the extent to which such activities might be justified and under what conditions.

9. To what extent is the present discussion applicable to the relations between nations? Is permanent peace possible, or is war inevitable?

19:   The Role of Religion

Is religion a help or a hindrance to morality?

The question sounds odd. Religion and morality are often equated, so that a religious person is assumed to be a moral person. Only a little more sophisticated is the attitude which looks on religion as an indispensable—or at least extremely helpful—bulwark of morality. How many tributes have been paid to "religion, the foundation of good citizenship and good conduct"? But the relationship between religion and morality is not that simple.

For one thing, it is obvious that there is no inevitable connection between religious belief and morally good behavior. People who hold very strong religious beliefs can commit moral atrocities. People with no identifiable religious convictions at all can lead morally exemplary lives. As we shall see, religious commitment can provide strong support for ethically correct behavior. But there is no necessary connection between the two things: being good and being religious are separate and distinct.

Furthermore, as we saw earlier, the effort to link religion to morality can have the unfortunate result of making religion the handmaid of ethics. In its simplest form this comes down to reducing religion to a single formula, "Be good or you won't go to heaven."

It may be true that being good (trying to do what one regards as morally right) is a precondition to going to heaven (achieving a permanently satisfactory relationship with the transcendent Other whom we call "God"), although that is beyond the scope of this discussion. But the trouble with the formulation is that it debases both salvation and goodness by making one the payoff for the other. In this way of looking at things religion and moral goodness are placed in the context of second-level (means-end) action rather than third-level action: action performed for its own sake in order to participate in a basic good.

At this point it is perhaps necessary to state something both obvious and important. In using words like "God," "religion," "heaven," "salvation," and so forth we are not departing from our established procedure and taking for granted the truth of religion in general or any one religion in particular. We are not taking it for granted that there is a God or that heaven exists—nor are we proposing to demonstrate the existence of either.

We are assuming that many of our readers will, in fact, have religious beliefs. If so, they will be interested in considering how ethics relates to such beliefs. Our purpose is simply to answer this question, How does, or should, religion relate to the subject matter of ethics? It is not necessary to assume the truth of religion in order to discuss the question.

Objections to religion

If the relationship of religion to ethics is not as cut-and-dried as many people believe, for others it is not obvious at all—or at least it is not obvious that there is any positive relationship between the two. On the contrary, many objections are raised to religion on ethical grounds. These say in different ways that not only does religion not necessarily foster good behavior but it actually hinders people in their efforts to do what is ethically right. Such objections generally take one of three forms.

First, it is said, by focusing man's attention on the transcendent—on God, salvation, heaven, the afterlife, and such—religion distracts him from the here and now and causes him to neglect his responsibilities to the world and the people around him. This is the argument advanced against supernatural religion by John Dewey and by Karl Marx ("religion is the opiate of the people"). Holding out the promise of happiness in a future life, religion seduces man from the task of correcting evils and injustices in this life.

It is nearly inevitable that religion should be open to this charge. As was suggested above, there is for all practical purposes no way to motivate a child—or a person who, while beyond childhood, is still morally immature—except by promising him a reward for acting in a certain way. In a religious context this naturally leads to the formulation "Be good or you won't go to heaven."

However, a true religious act is a third-level action—an act performed not simply to achieve a specific future objective (heaven, eternal life) but in order to participate in the good of religion now. A pattern of acts of this sort can be described as "living a holy life."

Notice that when one refers to an individual as "living a holy life," one speaks of him as doing something here and now. His action represents present participation in a good—in this case, the good of religion. So one might speak of another man as "living a scholarly life" (participating consistently in the good of truth or knowledge) or "living a sociable life" (participating consistently in the good of friendship).

Such expressions describe the pattern of life of persons who are not acting merely in order to achieve specific objectives but are instead participating consistently in certain goods. Thus, whatever else one might say of the individual who lives a holy life (that is, participates consistently in the good of religion), one at least cannot accuse him of ignoring the here and now; on the contrary, he is participating here and now in the good of religion, and doing so to such an extent that his manner of living can be characterized by the expression "living a holy life."

It may be objected that this still leaves him open to the accusation of ignoring other human goods. But if he is really doing what he is said to do—that is, participating consistently in the good of religion—this cannot be the case. As we have seen earlier, the reflexive goods, of which religion is one, are mutually dependent, so that to the degree a person acts contrary to one he is undermining his participation in all. Stated positively, this means that a person committed to and participating in one fundamental reflexive human good will also act, as far as he can, to realize the other reflexive human goods.

Furthermore, just as a basic commitment to one good—truth or friendship, for instance—does no more than constitute the framework within which the individual will work out his relationship to all the goods, so the man whose basic commitment is to the good of religion has merely established the emphasis and orientation of his life according to which he will seek to work out his relationship to all the other goods besides religion. A man who is really living a holy life has not cut himself off from everything else in human life except religion (any more than a man who is leading a scholarly life has cut himself off from everything else except knowledge); he has only established for himself the terms according to which everything else will be fitted into his life and he will relate to everything else.

Religion and freedom

A second objection to religion on ethical grounds is that religion destroys human freedom. According to religion, it is said, man is good if he is obedient to God's will; but to make man's goodness contingent on his obedience to God is to withdraw from him his autonomy and reduce him to a state of subjection. This complaint against religion is found in the work of a number of writers, notably Nietzsche, for whom it represents a major theme.

Like the first objection to religion, this one also is almost inevitable, given the necessity of presenting religious claims to children and to others who are morally immature. For such persons it is virtually inescapable that religious purposes and imperatives be presented as a system of rules to which obedience is demanded. Yet at the same time there exists in this an obvious danger: the danger of suggesting that the gulf between God and man is of the same sort as that between the exploiter and the exploited.

One solution to this difficulty—a false one—lies in asserting that religion makes no demands on anyone: religion has no connection with morality, is in fact fundamentally amoral. It is difficult to see, however, how such religion could contribute anything to achieving reconciliation between man and the transcendent. If there is a need for reconciliation, something must be *done* to effect it. This implies acting in certain ways, not acting in others.

A better solution to the objection is found in the fact that, as we have seen, responsibilities are not imposed externally on man but instead arise naturally from reality—from the reality of man himself. Man is not morally responsible because God arbitrarily wills it so. Rather, man has a responsibility to respect and seek to participate in human goods because it is humanly right and good to do so. A man who acts morally—as we have explained what it means to act morally—achieves fuller realization of his personhood by doing so; his humanity is enhanced, not debased.

Furthermore, even assuming a religious duty to do what God wills, the responsibilities associated with religion become moral responsibilities in precisely the same way as the moral responsibilities arising from any other basic human good. That is, the very moral responsibilities which arise from the good of religion are binding in the same way and for the same general reasons as the responsibilities which arise from the goods of truth and friendship: one has the responsibility of doing some things and not doing others because that is how one realizes more fully what it means to be human. If there is a God who commands us to do things, his commands are to be obeyed because what is commanded is humanly (in the deepest meaning of that word) right and good; it is simply not the case that what is commanded becomes right and good from the fact that God commands it.

Religion and evil

A third ethical objection to religion is based on the fact of evil: God cannot be both good and powerful or else he would not permit evil to exist. Some religious theories have attempted to answer this objection by speculating that God is in fact not powerful enough to prevent evil; on the contrary, it is suggested, the principle of good and the principle of evil are more or less coequal, and the struggle between them results sometimes in victory for one, sometimes in victory for the other.

A better solution to this problem emerges when one realizes that "good" has many different meanings, and there is no logical reason to suppose that our human understanding of what is good necessarily applies unequivocally to the transcendent being whom we call "God." It is unreasonable to attempt to measure divine action—or nonaction—according to the norms of human moral goodness.

Hypothetically, for example, God could be a utilitarian—because, presumably, an all-knowing being would possess the common denominator of goodness which is not accessible to human intelligence. To be sure, such an answer is extremely speculative, but the essential point is that it is simply unreasonable to try to apply simplistically a morality based on human goods to a being who is, by definition, nonhuman. One ought rather to take it for granted that what it means for God to be "good" will be radically different from what it means for a human being to be "good."

A variation on this objection is the assertion that religion itself has been and remains a force for evil in human life. Religion is an outlet for fanaticism, an occasion and excuse for men to act cruelly and unjustly toward their fellow men. This is an accusation leveled against religion by such writers as Voltaire, David Hume, and, in our own time, Bertrand Russell.

The impact of the indictment comes from the fact that it is true—although it is not the whole truth. A person can indeed practice fanaticism in the name of religion, for an exclusive (or exclusivistic) concentration on one category of human good—at the expense of others—is precisely what is meant by fanaticism. Just as there are fanatics in the pursuit of knowledge, fanatics in the pursuit of sensuality, fanatics in the pursuit of the whole range of human experiences, so too there are fanatics in the pursuit of religion.

There is, however, no necessary reason why religion should tend to breed fanaticism. Those who suggest otherwise mistake an abuse of religion for its entire reality. It is entirely possible to recognize a place for the human good of religion in one's life without making that particular good the absolute to which all else must be sacrificed. The good of religion is after all not identical with God, and even in traditional religious terms the quest for union with God is seen as involving the effort to respect and participate in many different goods besides those which lie in the category of religion.

In the Christian tradition even Christ, who according to orthodox faith is believed to be God made man, acted as man according to the conditions of human good. And the Christian must conform to God by conformity to Christ in his human nature. Christianity proposes that a man respond to the call to share intimately in divine life not by evading human responsibility—not by living inhumanly—but by fulfilling the requirements of what it means to be human. Christianity demands of its adherents that they be open to the fullness of human personhood, not that they be limited to the fanatical pursuit of one aspect or another.

Religion and hope

There is, however, more to be said about the relationship between ethics and religion than simply responding to various ethical objections to religion. On the contrary, there is or can be a positive relationship between the two, a relationship in which religion supports one in the effort to live a morally good life. To say this is not to assume the truth of religion, but only to point to the fact that hope, founded on traditional religious beliefs and attitudes, does in fact strongly buttress the effort of many people to do what is ethically right.

The key word here is "hope." And hope relates directly to the fact of evil.

Faced with the fact of evil in the world, one is tempted to respond in either of two ways: either with a kind of technological-humanistic presumption which takes for granted that, if only the proper techniques are found and applied, evil can be eradicated from human life; or with despair which takes for granted that evil is ineradicable and can never be fully overcome. The former attitude is illustrated by theories of progress and perfectibility, which deny freedom of self-determination, the sort of theories that are so prevalent in our Western culture, and which we have criticized over and over. The latter attitude is illustrated by theories of fatalism and rejection of the reality of the world, which also deny freedom of self-determination; these theories have been prevalent in Eastern cultures. Hope—a hope founded in religion—makes it possible to avoid either of these extremes.

Hope in this sense comes down to the conviction that doing what is right will not be fundamentally at odds with human well-being, even when doing what is right means refusing to do something which is wrong but which nevertheless seems to have humanly good consequences. This is of crucial importance, for it is obvious that doing what is right often does have painful consequences and that, on the contrary, there are frequently cases in which, humanly speaking and up to a point, immorality does pay.

Hope which is founded on religious belief enables us to cope with these facts and, in coping, to continue to do what is morally right. It does this by making it possible for us to believe that evil will ultimately be overcome, even though we cannot say how or when that will happen.

Only if one has such hope can one readily reject a morality of consequences, which holds that it is right to do evil so that good will come about. With such hope it is possible for one to say in effect, "Even though I do not see the good consequences of doing what is morally right in this difficult case, I will nevertheless do it, convinced that my responsibility as a free person is to do what is humanly good—to respect all of the human goods—not to achieve all humanly good consequences."

Religion in this sense is not a solution to man's moral predicament. It is not a panacea for the problem of evil—any more than psychoanalysis or social revolution or the latest theory of education is a panacea for this profound problem. If religion is regarded as a panacea, the result will be frustration; just as frustration will result if one looks to anything else as a panacea for moral evil. We are not presenting religion as a solution for evil; rather, we are pointing out that religion can be, has been, and still is a support for the effort of many people to do what is right in the face of evil.

Religion, and specifically Christian faith, places the paradox of moral evil in a perspective in which it is possible to live with it, neither rebelling nor despairing. To say that one can live with evil does not mean that one regards it complacently or fails to do what one can, consistent with the requirements of ethically good behavior, to correct and remove it. It means that one recognizes that because man is free, moral evil is and will continue to be a fact of human life, but in the context of religious belief it means further that one remains convinced that evil will ultimately be overcome, even though we do not know how this will come about.

Speaking now as persons who hold the Christian faith, we will add one further thought. Although Christ was a divine person, he willingly accepted the responsibilities of human freedom and thus demonstrated that this freedom is compatible with divine personhood. The implications of this fact for the individual Christian are enormous. Christianity not only allows but demands that a man approach the challenge of living with the intention of realizing as fully as he can all that it truly means to be human. Christianity need not stunt or degrade man; on the contrary, Christianity, understood as it really is, teaches mankind to respect the dignity of the human person and all that constitutes a person. And, finally, Christianity teaches that with God's help man's freedom will be able to fulfill the responsibilities that freedom entails.

Questions for review and discussion

1. To what extent do you think that, as a matter of historical fact, religion has distracted people from the here-and-now goods of this life?

2. Can you think of historical figures or people you know who you would say were really living holy lives and at the same time were committed to realizing human goods here and now?

3. Various types of religion have used various substantive goods as their vehicles. Show how life, aesthetic experience, play, and speculative knowledge have been vehicles for religion in various forms of it.

4. Can you think of examples in which substantive goods, serving as vehicles for religion, have been perverted to the status of mere means? Does the same thing also happen when other reflexive goods become the object of strong commitment?

5. Can you think of any reason why religion especially should give rise to fanaticism?

6. It has been said that the difference between a martyr and a fanatic is that a martyr is willing to die for what he believes in while a fanatic is willing to kill for what he believes in. Discuss.

7. Relate Augustine's conception of happiness, discussed in chapter three, to the fear that religion infringes on human freedom discussed in the present chapter.

8. Why do most people assume that God should act in a morally good way according to human standards of morality?

9. What is the difference between hope and optimism?

10. Do you agree that there is a relationship between religious conviction and the ability to resist utilitarianism? If so, do you think the relationship is the one sketched out here, or is there more to it than that?

20: We Must Decide Who We Shall Be

There are many possible life-styles which are good. Each of us must choose among them for himself. The choice is one that no one else can make for us.

Indeed, all of us must make many important decisions which profoundly shape our lives: whether or not to marry—and whom; what our occupation will be; where we shall live. It is true that such decisions are influenced and limited by circumstances over which we have no control. But it is also true that, for a normal individual in normal circumstances, such decisions do bring into play his freedom of self-determination.

These basic, life-determining choices concern the goods to which we shall devote ourselves and the communities in which we shall join with others in order to make our personal contribution to the common task of mankind. No one can set down hard-and-fast rules for making these basic decisions. But it is possible to offer some general suggestions.

To begin with, if we are to choose wisely we should try

to know ourselves as well as we can. This means discovering our capacities and special talents, and also recognizing and accepting our limitations. That does not imply committing oneself only to sure things—to small, limited goals that can be easily achieved. But it does require that we commit ourselves to purposes which we have a reasonable chance of realizing.

Even in the name of some higher good it would be unreasonable for a person who lacked the basic requirements of temperament and inclination to aspire to be a contemplative hermit. But it would be unworthy of a man probably endowed with the gifts of a concert pianist to settle down to a more certain career in an unchallenging line of work.

The myth of the well-rounded person

No one can really do everything well. But sometimes our culture pressures us to make the attempt. One of its enduring myths about self-determination and human development is focused on the ideal of the well-rounded person—the individual who is developed in all aspects.

The notion has its uses if it is not carried too far: if it means only that a person should not become so wrapped up in one area of endeavor that he completely neglects other matters to which he ought also to give attention (e.g., the job-oriented man who has no time to spare for sociability, recreation, or even intimacy with his family). But the myth of the well-rounded person becomes a pernicious thing when it involves people in the expenditure of tremendous amounts of time and energy in the effort to do a bit of everything—an effort whose usual result is that nothing is done really well.

Generous and altruistic people make this sort of mistake at least as easily as anyone else, and perhaps more readily than most. The classic do-gooder is into every cause and campaign, from civil rights to ecology, and often fails to make a significant contribution to any. Granted that there are many good causes in the world—many situations of evil and injustice which require redress—this does not mean that every person should become extensively involved in crusading on behalf of them all.

A person who is doing a successful job of teaching poor children how to read need not spread himself or herself thin by becoming intimately involved in consumer-protection campaigns—or vice versa. We must make choices; we must opt for certain areas of concentration in preference to others; and doing so is not only not bad, but positively good, if it makes it possible for us to do well something which is worth doing.

Making basic commitments

We should try to know as well as we can what possibilities are really open to us before choosing one or another. Too often even intelligent and well-educated people drift into extremely important commitments without a careful investigation of the alternatives and without consulting others who could help them deliberate wisely.

An obvious example is the careless way in which many people enter marriage—only to regret the decision as soon as the honeymoon is over if not before. It is no disparagement of romantic love, merely a recognition of its limitations as a basis for making sound choices, to say that two responsible people considering marriage will base their decision on other grounds in addition to the way they happen to feel about each other at the moment.

Having assessed our abilities and also the possibilities that are open to us, we should try to match our particular abilities to the possibilities we perceive. In doing this we should be quite deliberate and cautious (not the same thing, incidentally, as being merely timid and indecisive). In matters of fundamental importance one should never proceed simply on the basis of the information that happens to be readily available. We should reflect on ourselves and on the situation rather than simply following the bidding of imagination and feeling.

At the same time, though, we should take our feelings into account in this process of reflection, conscious that feelings often do mirror something important about our deeper selves. Usually we make a mistake if we try to force ourselves into a commitment contrary to our strong feelings. It is hard to be very optimistic about the prospects of a man who has had to force himself to become a doctor or a girl who has had to struggle against her emotions to bring herself to the point of saying "Yes" to a suitor.

In the matter of making commitments, however, a person should not be so excessively cautious as to make only safe choices and opt only for things which carry a "can't miss" label. One must indeed be willing to risk failure and the pain it brings with it, realizing that success—achieving what one has set out to do—is not essential to the morally good life and that failure by itself is not morally wrong.

Many good and important things, after all, have been accomplished only because some person or persons were willing to take the risk of failure. (Just as, of course, many people who have accepted this risk have actually failed— not indeed morally but in a practical sense.) From the point of view of ethics, it is not success or failure that determines goodness; it is commitment (or lack of commitment) to the realization of human goods, and action (or lack of action) to carry out this commitment.

How many commitments?

We must not make too many commitments. This does not mean "playing it cool," hanging back, and refusing to extend ourselves. There is nothing morally good about such an attitude. But it is also important to realize that every serious commitment carries with it serious moral responsibilities, responsibilities which often involve others besides ourselves. It is neither prudent nor good to take on so many such responsibilities that one is simply unable—for want of time or strength or talent—to satisfy them all, and must either neglect all of them to some extent or some of them entirely.

At the same time we should not fall into the trap of supposing that by accepting commitments we are somehow limiting our freedom (a notion put forward by Sartre). A freedom without content—which was in effect no more than a vague and unspecified openness to every sort of experience and activity without commitment to any—would be meaningless. We shape our lives and ourselves by the commitments we freely undertake. Refusal to make commitments is refusal to live as a person.

The responsibility each of us has to constitute his life—his self—is his own and no one else's. It is a serious mistake to allow this fundamental matter to be settled for us by the expectations (however benign) of others—parents, relatives, friends, the communities to which we belong, public opinion. We should listen to the counsel of others, but we must not let them make our fundamental decisions for us.

Altogether too many people, consciously or unconsciously, do in fact fulfill roles which have been pre-designed for them by others. The process by which this happens can be quite subtle, and considerable vigilance may be required to prevent its happening. At present, for example, popular culture in our society vehemently attacks role-playing, but that same culture simultaneously exerts powerful influences on individuals to conform to its standards and fit themselves to the roles it happens to approve. The potential for being victimized unawares in such circumstances is very great.

Each of us, in order to pull together the strands of his life and be a unified person, must make some most basic commitment which is broad enough to embrace all of his other commitments. Like a theme running through a piece of music, such a fundamental commitment gives coherence and pattern to what would otherwise be the disordered fragments of life.

If this commitment is to be made inclusivistically, it cannot be to one of the substantive goods (life, play, aesthetic experience, speculative knowledge) or to some part or aspect of these, because these goods cannot be realized in every act of our lives. That being so, the most basic, unifying commitment must be to one of the reflexive goods (integrity, authenticity, friendship, religion) which are, as we have seen, intrinsically connected, so that it is impossible to participate fully in any one of them without also being open to and participating in the others.

Even so, however, it is possible and indeed necessary that the emphasis of a person's most basic commitment be more on one of the reflexive goods than on the others. The others are not excluded; they simply take on a specific meaning—a special coloration, one might say—from the good to which the primary emphasis is given.

On which of these goods should an individual place the emphasis of his life? Harmony within the self (integrity) and between the self and one's action (authenticity) seem unsatisfactory choices, since such an emphasis would tend to have the practical outcome of subordinating others to oneself. Friendship and justice, important as they are, also seem inappropriate choices, because this orientation would tend to have the effect of subordinating oneself to others.

That leaves religion—and religion seems indeed the best choice to receive the emphasis of one's most basic commitment in life. To the extent that we identify the transcendent Other with the principle which sustains human goods, even when they are not chosen, making one's religious commitment most fundamental is closely related to—if not identical with—taking one's moral stand on the side of openness to all of the human goods. Emphasis upon this good can fulfill the need for integration of the person, without in any way constricting or devaluating one's proper concern for harmony within one's self and with one's neighbor.

We have come, then, to the end of this discussion, and we find that we are in a sense back at the point from which we began. The fundamental responsibility of human freedom is the responsibility faced by each person to create his own life, his own self, through the choices he makes. We can use this freedom well or badly, but we cannot avoid using it. Using freedom well means choosing in ways that progressively open us to ever-greater realization of what it means to be a human person; using freedom badly means choosing in ways that limit and eventually kill our capacity for further growth.

Ethics, far from being a stereotyped set of do's and don't's, is an effort on the part of human reason to provide guidelines for making choices which make possible our continued growth as human persons. Only when we choose in this way and continue to grow as persons can we truly be called "happy."

Such happiness is not the same as gratification or practical success. To live in a morally good way is always more or less difficult, almost inevitably involves us in pain, and may enmesh us in tragedy—if "tragedy" is defined as failure to achieve limited goals and objectives. This, however, is the reality and the dignity of human life. Freedom is both blessing and burden—in both respects it lies at the heart of what it means to be human.

Questions for review and discussion

1. Does the view that there are many different life-styles from which to choose admit an element of subjectivism or relativism into this ethics?

2. Why must good people not be conformists?

3. Why do you think the ideal of the well-rounded person has taken such strong hold on the thinking of many people?

4. Should counseling help people avoid drifting into important commitments without sufficient consideration? Has it done so for you or for people whom you know?

5. To what extent do you take your feelings into account when making important decisions? Of all the emotions which ones do you think it most important to pay attention to?

6. Do you think your friends and acquaintances are sufficiently willing to risk failure in life, or are they more likely to settle for greater security for themselves rather than run risks for important human goods?

7. Some people make basic commitments in life mainly due to adolescent rebellion. For instance, they get married because their parents are against it. Others make their basic commitments too much under the influence of others—for example, by entering a certain profession because their family has always planned that this is what they should do. What signs would characterize a commitment which is really personal and which is not unduly influenced in either of these directions?

8. Do you agree that it is necessary to have some overarching commitment which organizes and harmonizes all the other basic commitments of one's life? If so, do you think we are correct in suggesting that this should be a commitment to the religious purpose? Is it possible for a good person to integrate his life in some other way?

Suggestions for Further
Reading and Research

These suggestions are not intended as a general bibliography for the field of ethics. Many of the topics we treat are discussed in articles in the *Encyclopedia of Philosophy;* these articles usually introduce various positions on a topic and provide rather extensive bibliography. R. B. Brandt, *Ethical Theories: The Problems of Normative and Critical Ethics* (Englewood Cliffs, N.J.: Prentice-Hall, 1959), summarizes and criticizes many ethical theories and provides very good bibliographies. W. T. Jones, Frederick Sontag, M. O. Beckner, and R. J. Fogelin, eds., *Approaches to Ethics*, 2nd ed. (New York: McGraw-Hill, 1969) is a good collection of selections from major philosophic works in ethics from Plato to the present. Vernon J. Bourke, *History of Ethics* (Garden City, N.Y.: Doubleday, 1968), is an excellent, up-to-date history of ethics; this work is also available (1970) in two paperback volumes. T. E. Hill, *Contemporary Ethical Theories* (New York: Macmillan, 1951), briefly treats almost all current theories.

Philip B. Rice, *Our Knowledge of Good and Evil* (New York: Random House, 1955), includes a useful summary and critique of the many positions developed in Anglo-American ethics from about 1900-1950. Henry B. Veatch, *For an Ontology of Morals: A Critique of Contemporary Ethical Theory* (Evanston: Northwestern U. Press, 1971), systematically criticizes contemporary theories and points in

209

the direction of an ethics something like ours; Veatch's book could be a useful introduction to ours for the more advanced reader.

Our discussion of freedom in chapter one owes much to, but freely departs from, Mortimer J. Adler, *The Idea of Freedom: A Dialectical Examination of the Conception of Freedom*, 2 vols. (Garden City, N.Y.: Doubleday, 1958 and 1961). Karl R. Popper, *Of Clouds and Clocks: An Approach to the Problem of Rationality and the Freedom of Man* (St. Louis: Washington U., 1966), appraises the relation between contemporary physics and human freedom of self-determination. Joseph M. Boyle, Jr., Germain Grisez, and Olaf Tollefsen, "Determinism, Freedom, and Self-Referential Arguments," *Review of Metaphysics*, 26 (Sept. 1972), pp. 3-37, develops in a technical form the argument that determinism is self-referentially inconsistent. Austin Farrer, *The Freedom of the Will* (London: Adam & Charles Block, 1958), esp. pp. 132-139, develops the point that in practice one must think and act on the supposition of freedom.

Hannah Arendt, *The Human Condition* (Chicago and London: U. of Chicago Press, 1958), pp. 79-247, distinguishes labor, work, and action—roughly corresponding to our first-, second-, and third-level action. Gabriel Marcel, *Being and Having: An Existential Diary* (New York: Harper & Row, 1965), pp. 154-174, distinguishes being and having—roughly corresponding to our third and second levels of action, respectively. Aristotle, *Nichomachean Ethics*, book 6, distinguishes between art and prudence—roughly corresponding to our second and third levels of action, respectively. John Dewey, *Reconstruction in Philosophy* (Boston: Beacon, 1957), pp. 161-170, presents a version of situation ethics. Joseph Fletcher, *Situation Ethics: The New Morality* (Philadelphia: Westminster, 1966), pp. 26-31, 134-145, treats the situation as determinant of morality.

Mortimer J. Adler, *The Time of Our Lives: The Ethics of Common Sense* (New York: Holt, Rinehart, and Winston, 1970), pp. 3-63, sees the ethical problem as one of giving meaning to life; he does not distinguish second- and third-level action sharply, but does (pp. 86-97) explain that neither pleasure nor a technical end can give meaning to life. St. Augustine, *City of God*, book 19, presents the classic doctrine of heaven as principle of meaning for human life. Germain G. Grisez, "Man, the Natural End of," *New Catholic Encyclopedia*, vol. 9, pp. 132-138, criticizes traditional conceptions of man's natural end. Vatican Council II, *The Church in the Modern World*, part 1, chap. 3, moderates the Augustinian emphasis on heaven as future, stresses that the kingdom of God is already present in mystery.

Our references to Aristotle in chapter four are to *Nichomachean Ethics*, books 1 and 10. Henry B. Veatch, *Rational Man: A Modern Interpretation of Aristotelian Ethics* (Bloomington: Indiana U. Press, 1964), pp. 148-154, introduces freedom, which alters Aristotle's position in the direction of ours. Gabriel Marcel, *Creative Fidelity*, trans. Robert Rosthal (New York: Farrar, Straus, 1964), pp. 104-119, presents the life of a person as a unique act. Charles Fried, *An Anatomy of Values: Problems of Personal and Social Choice* (Cambridge, Mass.: Harvard U. Press, 1970), pp. 87-101, introduces the concept of "life plan" and considers life as an ordered set of rational acts. John Rawls, *A Theory of Justice* (Cambridge, Mass.: Harvard U. Press, 1971), pp. 551-567, argues against hedonism and against any theory that tries to reduce the human good to a single good.

Our treatment of community in chapter five owes much to, but freely departs from, Aristotle, *Nichomachean Ethics*, book five (justice) and books eight and nine (friendship); the distinction between friendship of utility and friendship based on virtue corresponds to our distinction between contract and community. Charles Fried, in the work already cited, pp. 105-115, outlines a concept of society similar to our idea of community. Yves R. Simon, *Philosophy of Democratic Government* (Chicago & London: U. of Chicago Press, 1951), deals with democratic society as a potential form of community; Simon is especially helpful for his treatment of the problem of authority.

A classic statement of the subjectivism we discuss in chapter six is Bertrand Russell, *Human Society in Ethics and Politics* (London: Allen & Unwin; Simon & Schuster, 1955). A good example of relativism is W. G. Sumner, *Folkways* (Boston: Ginn, 1934). J. D. Mabbott, *An Introduction to Ethics* (Garden City, N.Y.: Doubleday, 1969), pp. 70-102, criticizes subjectivism. Peter A. Bertocci and Richard M. Millard, *Personality and the Good: Psychological and Ethical Perspectives* (New York: David McKay, 1963), pp. 260-294, criticize relativism and subjectivism. Vernon J. Bourke, *Ethics in Crisis* (Milwaukee: Bruce, 1966), pp. 102-119, takes up the problem of objective values in light of recent work in anthropology. Morris Ginsberg, *On the Diversity of Morals* (London: Mercury Books, 1962), pp. 26-40, 97-129, criticizes cultural relativism. Abraham Edel, *Ethical Judgment: The Use of Science in Ethics* (Glencoe, Ill.: Free Press, 1955), criticizes relativism; out of this develops the concept of a "valuational base" (pp. 297-310), the content of which is what we attempt to formulate in chapter seven.

Also relevant to chapter seven is a tentative analysis of human needs by Bertocci and Millard, in their work already cited, pp. 157-172. A. H. Maslow, *Motivation and Personality* (New York: Harper & Row, 1954), pp. 80-106, gives a psychologist's approach to basic needs roughly corresponding to our fundamental purposes. William K. Frankena, *Ethics*, 2nd ed. (Englewood Cliffs, N.J.: Prentice-Hall, 1973), p. 88, gives a list similar to but longer than our list of intrinsic goods.

Erich Fromm, *Man for Himself* (New York: Rinehart, 1947), presents a theory of human goodness which reduces it to health. Thomas Aquinas, *Truth*, vol. 3, trans. R. W. Schmidt (Chicago: Henry Regnery, 1954), question 21, presents a tight treatise on *good*, which really amounts to an entire value theory. Germain Grisez, "The First Principle of Practical Reason: A Commentary on the *Summa theologiae*, 1-2, Question 94, Article 2," *Natural Law Forum*, vol. 10 (1965), pp. 168-201, a technical expression of our value theory, with some critique of alternatives.

Chapter nine's treatment of the basic principle of morality has few parallels in other literature. Among the few are Rudolf Allers, *The Psychology of Character*, trans. E. B. Strauss (London & New York: Sheed & Ward, 1933), pp. 206-240, which represents "true and false ideals" of character corresponding to our distinction, but in psychological terms. Joseph de Finance, S. J., *Essai sur l'agir humain* (Rome: Université Grégorienne, 1962), pp. 304-348, locates moral value in the openness of free commitment to the transcendent, moral disvalue in closedness upon a particular value.

The utilitarianism discussed in chapter ten received a classic formulation in Jeremy Bentham, *An Introduction to the Principles of Morals and Legislation* (New York: Hefner, 1948), pp. 1-42. Also John Stuart Mill, *Utilitarianism* (New York: Library of the Liberal Arts, 1954). John Dewey develops his situationism in the work already cited, pp. 161-170. Joseph Fletcher's work already cited is his fullest expression of his theory; Fletcher was criticized very effectively by Paul Ramsey, *Deeds and Rules in Christian Ethics* (New York: Charles Scribners' Sons, 1967), pp. 145-225. A book-length critique of utilitarianism is David Lyons, *Forms and Limits of Utilitarianism* (Oxford: Clarendon Press, 1965). A brief critique of utilitarianism and outline of the present theory: Germain Grisez, "Methods of Ethical Inquiry," *Proceedings of the American Catholic Philosophical Association*, vol. 41 (1967), pp. 160-168.

Many works could be cited to illustrate the philosophic development of one or another of the modes of responsibility in chapter eleven. John Rawls, in the work already cited, pp. 407-433 (and see works referred to p. 408) presents a position similar to the first mode of responsibility. R. M. Hare, *Freedom and Reason* (New York: Oxford U. Press, 1965), builds his ethics on the second mode of responsibility, which had its classic treatment in Immanuel Kant, *Foundations of the Metaphysics of Morals*, trans. Lewis White Beck (Indianapolis: Library of Liberal Arts, 1959), p. 50, and *passim*. An ancient work, Epictetus, *Discourses*, bases ethics on the fourth mode of responsibility. Josiah Royce, *The Philosophy of Loyalty* (New York: Macmillan, 1908), develops an admirable balance of the fourth and fifth modes; he also has a good understanding of the idea of commitment, and his thinking is not far from the idea of openness to all goods as a criterion of morality. Gabriel Marcel, *Creative Fidelity* (previously cited), pp. 147-174, deals with the fifth mode.

Chapter twelve's treatment of duties can be supplemented by close study of Aristotle, *Nichomachean Ethics*, book 5 (justice). An ethics of duty is F. H. Bradley, *Ethical Studies* (Indianapolis, New York: Library of Liberal Arts, 1951), esp. pp. 98-112. Current points of view are represented in J. A. Bedau, ed., *Justice and Equality* (Englewood Cliffs, N.J.: Prentice-Hall, 1971).

Chapter thirteen's treatment of the eighth mode of responsibility will be illustrated in the concise traditional statement of Thomas Aquinas, *Summa theologiae*, 1-2, question 20, article 2. Eric d'Arcy, *Human Acts: An Essay in Their Moral Evaluation* (Oxford: Clarendon Press, 1963), does not go as far as we do, but presents an analysis helpful as far as he goes. Germain Grisez, *Abortion: The Myths, the Realities, and the Arguments* (New York and Cleveland: Corpus Books, 1970), pp. 307-346, applies the ideas treated in chapters thirteen and fourteen to abortion.

A more technical and historical treatment of the problem of chapter fourteen is Germain Grisez, "Toward a Consistent Natural-Law Ethics of Killing," *American Journal of Jurisprudence and Legal Philosophy*, vol. 15 (1970), pp. 64-96. R. A. Wassertrom, ed., *War and Morality* (Belmont, California: Wadsworth, 1970), essays on war from various viewpoints.

Chapter fifteen will be supplemented by Eliseo Vivas, *The Moral Life and the Ethical Life* (Chicago: U. of Chicago Press, 1950), pp. 185-267, who treats the person as constituted by free commitment to objective values. Abraham H. Maslow, *Toward a Psychology of Being*, 2nd ed. (New York: Von Nostrand Reinhold Co., 1968), pp.

149-185, gives a psychological account of establishing self-identity that parallels our ethical account; note his treatment of values as objective potentialities. Erik Erikson, *Insight and Responsibility* (New York: W. W. Norton, 1964), pp. 83-134, another psychological account close to our view; his wholeness/totality distinction corresponds to our inclusivity/exclusivity distinction.

Chapter sixteen owes something to G. C. de Menasce, *The Dynamics of Morality* (New York: Sheed & Ward, 1961), a remarkable effort to show how human goods provide sufficient reason to *be* good. Our educational theory is closest to that of Montessori; see E. M. Standing, *Maria Montessori: Her Life and Work* (New York, Toronto: New American Library, 1962), esp. chapter 17, for an introduction.

Chapter seventeen on progress draws upon, but departs from, Charles van Doren, *The Idea of Progress* (New York: Praeger, 1967), which has a survey of theories of progress. John Passmore, *The Perfectibility of Man* (New York: Charles Scribner's Sons, 1970), offers a full critique of moral progress theories; we do not consider him always fair to religious views. Herbert Spencer, *Illustrations of Universal Progress* (New York: Appleton, 1889), illustrates evolutionary optimism. A sympathetic presentation of Marxist views is John Somerville, *The Philosophy of Marxism: An Exposition* (New York: Random House, 1967), pp. 121-159.

Chapter eighteen may be supplemented by Michael Walzer, *Obligation: Essays on Disobedience, War, and Citizenship* (Cambridge, Mass.: Harvard U. Press, 1970), who discusses problems of revolution and reform, and related issues, in an ethical context based on the concept of social responsibility as communitarian. Norman Cohn, *The Pursuit of the Milennium* (New York: Harper & Row, 1961), pp. 307-319, sums up the implications of history for the idea that revolution is a panacea. Hannah Arendt, *The Origins of Totalitarianism* (New York: Meridian, 1958), pp. 460-479, develops the idea of ideology in relation to efforts to transform man radically. Lewis A. Feuer, *The Conflict of Generations: The Character and Significance of Student Movements* (New York, London: Basic Books, 1969), offers a historical and psychological study of student movements, suggesting much of their energy is wasted. H. L. A. Hart, *The Concept of Law* (Oxford: Clarendon Press, 1961); and Lon L. Fuller, *The Morality of Law*, rev. ed. (New Haven, London: Yale U. Press, 1969) present philosophies of law based on contrasting ideas of the national community. The two authors think they disagree, but Hart's theory emphasizes the contract aspect of civil society while Fuller's theory attends to its community aspect; the two together give a quite adequate understanding of what law is.

Chapter nineteen's reference to Nietzsche can be illustrated in Friedrich Nietzsche, *The Portable Nietzsche*, ed. Walter Kaufmann (New York: Viking, 1954), pp. 197-200. E. H. Madden and P. H. Hare, *Evil and the Concept of God* (Springfield, Ill.: Thomas, 1968), state and develop the objections based on evil. James F. Ross, *Introduction to the Philosophy of Religion* (New York: Macmillan, 1969), provides tight philosophical arguments for setting aside some of these objections. Gabriel Marcel, *Homo Viator: Introduction to a Metaphysic of Hope* (New York: Harper & Row, 1965), pp. 29-67, develops the concept of hope. Vincent Punzo, *Reflective Naturalism: an Introduction to Moral Philosophy* (New York: Macmillan, 1969), pp. 315-368, deals with ethical objections to religion and suggests a role for religion in moral life similar to our hope. Bertocci and Millard, in the work already cited, pp. 677-697, present a somewhat similar view; Punzo is Catholic; Bertocci and Millard are not.

Chapter twenty's reference to Sartre can be verified in Jean-Paul Sartre, *Being and Nothingness: An Essay on Phenomenological Ontology*, trans. Hazel E. Barnes (New York: Philosophical Library, 1956), pp. 464-481. Dietrich von Hildebrand, *Christian Ethics* (New York: David McKay, 1953), pp. 161-166 and 453-463, deals with religious commitment as basic in life.

Index

217